The Alaskan CampCook

ALASKA NORTHWEST PUBLISHING COMPANY
Anchorage, Alaska

Printed in U.S.A.

First Printing, March 1963
Second Printing, October 1968
Third Printing, August 1973
Fourth Printing, June 1976

Illustrations by Rie Munoz, Juneau, Alaska
Cover Photo by Jim Rearden, Homer, Alaska

LIBRARY OF CONGRESS CATALOG NUMBER: 62-22307
International Standard Book No. 0-88240-000-2

HERE is a land (Alaska) rich in natural bounty. We have more big game, more fish, and more relatively virgin wilderness than any other state of the United States. The creatures which live in our land and the things which grow here are treasures we cherish.

But if we are to assure that these things we cherish shall obtain tomorrow and for posterity we must cultivate the principles of good sportsmanship, and as sportsmen we must labor in unison to this end.

The organized sportsmen of Alaska and their wives and friends pooled recipes to make this uniquely Alaskan cook book possible. It has been our pleasure to edit and publish. For every book sold, a percentage of returns will be given to the Alaska Sportsmen's Council to further that organization's efforts.

For all of us it has been a labor of love – not merely for the pleasures of eating, but for this wonderful Alaska of ours so blessed with nature's riches. As you share our cooking secrets, so also may you share this love of ours for Alaska.

Sincerely,

Robert A. Henning

Robert A. Henning
Editor & Publisher
ALASKA® magazine

Contents

Chapter 8

FISH

Chapter 9

SHELLFISH

Chapter 10

WILD FRUIT

Chapter 11

THE RED VACCINIUMS

Chapter 12

WILD VEGETABLES

Chapter 13

SOURDOUGH

HARLEQUIN
MALLARD
BRANT
PINTAIL
BLUEBILL

Chapter **1**

DUCK AND GOOSE

How to Dress Game Birds

Bleed bird by sticking a sharp knife down the throat to sever the main artery, and hang bird head down until bleeding stops. Remove crop and entrails as soon as possible, though feathers may be left on without spoiling the flavor. If not cleaned when caught, birds should be dressed as soon as they arrive in camp. To leave birds undrawn results in poorly flavored meat.

To remove feathers, dip in hot but not boiling water and pick most of the feathers. Melt 2 pounds paraffin over hot water. Roll birds in melted paraffin. Dip in ice water. When the wax hardens, peel it off and all the rest of the feathers will come off with the wax. Skin ducks and small birds if they are hard to pluck.

Leave birds whole for roasting, but for frying cut apart at the joints. Small birds have so little meat on legs and wings that sometimes only the breasts are served. Other portions may be boiled for soup.

University of Alaska Agricultural Extension Service

Roast Duck or Goose, Baked Duck

Wipe the cleaned bird dry and cut away loose fat. Stuff with any poultry dressing, wild rice dressing, or a fruit dressing of soaked prunes and dried apples. Skewer or sew the openings. Place ducks in an open pan in a very hot oven and bake 20 to 25 minutes. Baste every 5 minutes with water and melted butter. Serve rare—pink juice oozes out.

Roast goose in a slow oven (300-325°) until well done, allowing 18 to 20 minutes per pound. For duck, roast in a moderate oven (325-350°) for 1 to 2½ hours. Cover with greased cloth or bacon strips as it roasts to keep the skin moist. Bird is done when legs are loose and skin is nicely browned.

U. of A. AES

Roasting goose in a brown paper bag saves cleaning the oven. Several holes in the bottom of the bag allow grease to drain out, and bird browns nicely without basting.

Louise Juhnke, Chugiak

Duck Hints

If you suspect your duck has been feeding on fish, give him a decent burial and forget him. You cannot destroy that fishy flavor with any kind of treatment.

Soaking a duck in salt water, vinegar, soda water or what-have-you will do nothing for the duck. If you enjoy the gamey flavor of duck, respect it. If not, eat something else.

Never skin a duck. You don't need to eat the skin, but it helps retain the natural juices of the bird.

Stuffing is used in ducks primarily for flavor; hence it is highly seasoned. It serves to draw out and subdue some of the wild taste, and is discarded.

In roasting, always place ducks on their breasts, turning over the last half hour. This keeps the breast meat moist.

Henrietta Power, Juneau

Alaska Wild Duck Supreme

Dress and clean wild duck thoroughly. Split down the backbone. Soak duck in Burgundy wine 2 hours, allowing 1 pt. wine for each duck. Turn frequently so all parts are well marinated.

Remove from wine, season well, rubbing salt and pepper inside. Stuff each duck with raw potato, apple and onion. Tie or sew securely. Place in Dutch oven, pour the wine over it, cover and cook in 400° oven until thoroughly done, basting frequently. To brown the meat, remove cover 20 minutes before taking from the oven.

Remove string and discard potato, onion and apple.

Ruth C. Allman, Juneau

Roast Wild Duck

Pick duck dry, or dip in hot (not boiling) water until water penetrates to skin. Grasp feathers close to skin and pull in direction feathers grow, not against it. Cut off wing tips. Dress duck and rub inside and out with salt and pepper. Place medium-sized onion or small apple in craw and fill cavity with your favorite bread or rice stuffing. Truss, place in greased roaster breast side down (uncovered) in moderate oven (350°) until light brown. Turn duck on back and brush breast with fat.

Allow 15 minutes per pound for young duck, 20 minutes for old ducks. Increase heat to 450° for final browning if desired.

If you like the "gamey" flavor, roast young, tender duck whole or split in half, in 450° oven for no longer than 15 to 20 minutes—just long enough to get a crisp brown crust.

Teen Cox, Skagway

Wild Duck, Oven-Fried

Pick, clean, wash and dry the duck. Disjoint, cut out wishbone, cut breast and back in half. Dredge with seasoned flour. Brown lightly on all sides in a heavy skillet or Dutch oven with a little fat. Add one can consommé and about ¼ can water.

Cover and place in a moderate oven (300 to 350°) for about an hour. Add more water if needed to prevent cooking dry. Just before serving, thicken liquid slightly and serve as gravy with cooked wild rice. A little wine may be added to the consommé and water if you have it handy.

Quick-Fried Breast of Duck

Lay uncleaned duck on its back. Slit skin from edge of crop to back end of breast bone. Pull skin sidewise to side of breast meat. Loosen breasts

OLD SQUAW DUCKS
CANADA GEESE
GROUSE
CANVASBACK DUCK

along the breast bone and remove whole.

Cut breast meats across the grain in strips about ½ inch thick.

Fry some bacon until nearly done. Place strips of breast in bacon grease and fry to suit. Pour the bacon, duck and drippings on hot cakes and dispose of in the usual manner. (Caution to guides and hunters escorting cheechakoes: Don't try this dish on your guests. They'll want it every meal!)

G. R. Gray, Haines

Duck Stew

Clean duck left after preparing above recipe, cut in suitable pieces, place in stew pot with onions and cover with plenty of water. Salt and pepper to taste. Bring to medium boil and cook about 1 hour. Add stiff dumplings made of hot cake mix, and continue boiling for about 4 minutes in covered pot. (Less time may be needed for dumplings in fast boil.)

G. R. Gray, Haines

Roast Duck with Wild Rice Dressing

To 2/3 cup boiling water add 1/3 cup wild rice. Reduce heat and simmer gently until rice is done and liquid absorbed, about 1 hour.

In a small amount of butter saute: 1 small onion, minced; 1/3 cup finely chopped celery; 1/3 cup minced green pepper. Add this mixture, plus 2 tbsp. sherry and ½ tsp. salt, to rice.

Sprinkle dressed bird inside and out with salt and pepper. Rub skin with a light sprinkling of garlic salt. Stuff bird with rice mixture. Place in shallow pan, without rack, and in 350° oven.

Making a basting sauce of ½ cube butter, ¼ cup sherry and ¼ tsp. poultry seasoning, heated to the boiling point. Baste occasionally.

Roast birds until done—two hours more or less depending upon size and age of birds.

The above amount of dressing is ample for one mallard. The basting sauce is enough for two ducks of mallard size, but should be increased slightly for more than two birds.

Mrs. Sam H. Roberson, Douglas

Roast Wild Duck or Goose

Dress ducks or geese immediately after killing. Soak in water for 3 or 4 hours. Dry and place in cool spot for 2 days or longer. Wash well again before cooking. Place mixture of celery, carrots, apple and orange in body cavity and rings of orange over breast. Bake in slow oven until birds are tender and brown. When nearly cooked, add water and sherry and baste birds with liquor in cooking pan. The stuffing is for flavor and is discarded before serving. Thicken liquor in pan and serve with birds.

Mrs. Rudy Sarvela, Sitka

Ducks Philippine

Cut up and dredge a couple of ducks in flour to which ½ tsp. salt has been added. Brown the pieces in hot fat with one sliced onion. Remove from pan and line same pan with fresh orange slices. Lay duck pieces thereon. Pour over all 1 cup orange juice. Cover. Simmer on top of stove 1 to 1½ hours, or cook in slow oven (300-325°).

Mrs. Urban C. Nelson, Juneau

Duck or Goose Too Old to Fry

If you have a duck or goose that may be a little tough, try this method:

Cut the bird into serving pieces. Dredge with flour and salt. Brown in hot fat. Put browned pieces in greased casserole with 1 sliced onion. Pour over this 1 can of thick white apple juice. Bake in casserole, covered, very slowly (275-300°) for several hours. Makes a tender morsel out of a tough old bird!

Mrs. Urban C. Nelson, Juneau

Wild Goose or Duck Roasted Without Stuffing

Pick and clean the birds. Soak overnight in cold water to which has been added 2 tbsp. vinegar and 1 tbsp. salt. Drain. Salt and pepper inside and out. Fill cavity with chopped onions, minced garlic and outside stalks or leaves of celery. Place in a roasting pan. Beside the bird put a bay leaf and a few pieces of rosemary. Roast geese in a slow oven (300-325°) until well done, allowing 18 to 20 minutes per pound. Roast ducks in a moderate oven (325-350°) for 1 to 2½ hours.

U. of A. AES

Braised Duck

Skin and cut up ducks into serving pieces. Season with salt and pepper and dredge with flour. Brown in hot fat. Place in roaster. Brown generous amount of minced onion and green pepper in drippings. Add water and pour over all the ducks. Cover and cook in slow oven (325°) until tender.

Mrs. Clayton L. Polley, Juneau

Duck in the Mud

While you are having breakfast, build up a good campfire in a hollow. Your duck or goose is eviscerated, so wipe out clean with a cloth. Rub the inside thoroughly with salt and a little pepper. Stuff cavity with an apple, an onion or both. Fold the feathers to cover all openings and plaster the whole thing with a coat of clay mud (sand or loam will not do) about an inch thick. Place the bird in the bottom of your fire among the ashes and cover well with wood. Go hunting all day, and when you return for dinner, be prepared for the best duck or goose you ever tasted. Dig it out of the ashes (it should still be hot) and break off the clay. The feathers come with it.

Kenneth Hughes, Haines

Black Coot Ducks

If you're stuck in the woods or on the beach and the meat supply is nil, try this with "fish" ducks: Skin out the breasts of 3 coots. Soak in salt-water and vinegar for 3 hours. Dry and dredge with flour. Brown in bacon fat. Add a large onion chopped up, salt and pepper, and enough water to simmer as for pot roast. Add 1 tsp. mixed spices. When nearly done add 1 cup red wine (if available) and let simmer until done. Thicken the liquor for gravy.

Mrs. E. E. Weschenfelder, Fritz Cove

Pot Roast Wild Goose

After hanging the goose for a day or so, clean it thoroughly, wiping out the cavity with a rag wrung out of vinegar. Season the inside with 1 tsp. salt and ½ tsp. pepper. Stuff with two peeled and sliced apples, a sliced carrot, a whole onion and three or four celery stalks. Or fill the cavity with your own favorite dressing. Sew the opening together with stout thread and tie the wings and legs to the body. Rub the outside of the goose with butter seasoned with salt and pepper.

Brown in melted butter in a heavy skillet. When the goose is evenly browned on all sides, add about 2 cups of water, cover, and cook slowly until tender—about two hours.

Fried or Broiled Grouse or Ptarmigan

Split the cleaned bird down the back and press pieces flat. Brush with oil and sprinkle with salt. Place skin-side down and broil 15 minutes, turning once. Place strip of bacon on each bird and broil until bacon is crisp. If desired, baste every 5 minutes with barbecue sauce or sweet pickle juice. Before serving, sprinkle with paprika.

Disjoint larger birds (and rabbits) and fry like chicken in fat. A quick method is to cut meat from the bones in chunks or slices, and dredge with flour, salt and pepper by shaking in a paper bag. Fry in fat 15 minutes, to a golden-brown. Pressure-cook bones 10 minutes to make soup or gravy.

U. of A. AES

Ptarmigan en Casserole

- 2 ptarmigan (about 1¼ lbs. each), dressed
- 5 tbsp. butter
- Peel of ½ orange
- Peel of ½ lemon
- 1 doz. juniper berries
- ¼ cup white wine
- 2 tbsp. burnt brandy

Sear birds in 3 tbsp. butter, turning constantly until golden brown—about 20 minutes. Then place in casserole with butter from frying pan, adding 2 tbsp. more melted butter, orange and lemon peel, and juniper berries. Sprinkle with wine and cook in a slow oven 15 minutes, basting lightly. Just before serving, lift the ptarmigan out of the casserole and put a little burnt brandy on top of the birds. Cover with the gravy. Yield, 2 to 4 portions.

U. of A. AES

Ptarmigan Breasts Fried

Pluck and clean the ptarmigan. Remove the breast meat from bone with a sharp knife. Place pieces on a plate, sprinkle with salt, pepper, garlic salt, 2 or 3 drops of soy sauce on each piece, and about ½ tsp. salad oil or melted shortening of some kind. Let meat sit for an hour.

Dip breast pieces in flour or a mixture of flour and cracker crumbs. Melt some fat in a heavy skillet, brown ptarmigan breasts on both sides. Add a small amount of water, cover with heavy lid and let steam about 20 minutes or until tender.

Gussie and Bill Byington, Juneau

Grouse Fricassee

Pluck and clean the grouse. Cut into several pieces, salt and pepper, add onion or garlic salt if you like the flavor. Roll each piece of meat in flour until heavily coated. Brown each piece in fat in a heavy skillet. Pour on about ½ cup water, cover and let simmer about an hour or until tender.

When ready to serve, remove the meat, add 2 tbsp. flour to pan, stir to blend, add 1 cup milk and salt and pepper to taste.

Gussie and Bill Byington, Juneau

Grouse Mulligan

- 1 good-sized onion, sliced
- 1 clove garlic
- 1 green pepper
- Salt, pepper, flour, grouse

Cut up bird, roll in flour and brown in hot drippings. Season with salt and pepper and put into a covered baking dish. Slice the onion, put it, the green pepper and garlic over the meat, add a cup of hot water. Cook at least 2 hours in a slow oven (about 350°). Add more water while cooking, if necessary. (I dredge a little flour over it once or twice during the cooking.)

This is a good way to use old birds, but young grouse should be fried the same as chicken. If your hunter brings in only one grouse, and it isn't enough for the family, try adding 1 lb. veal stew meat, browned and cooked the same as the bird. The veal cuts the wild taste of the bird somewhat, as well as increasing the amount of meat.

Lulu MacKechnie,
PTA COOK BOOK, Petersburg

Ptarmigan and Dumplings

Use breasts, and legs if meaty, of two or three birds, depending upon number and capacity of people eating. Flour pieces and brown in skillet with giblets and an onion if desired. Season to taste. (I use salt, pepper, garlic powder and sometimes a touch of thyme.) Add water to cover and simmer 2 hours. Make dumplings with 1 cup flour, 2 tsp. baking powder, ½ tsp. salt and liquid enough to make a soft dough. Drop gently, a teaspoonful at a time, on ptarmigan, cover and cook 15 minutes more.

Good, too, with mashed potatoes or boiled rice instead of dumplings.

Georgia Griffin, Fairbanks

CARIBOU
MOOSE

Chapter **2**

MOOSE, CARIBOU, VENISON

To Bleed and Dress Out

Approach fallen animal cautiously from the rear in case it is not dead. Place knee on its neck and reach over to locate the soft spot between neck and breastbone, plunge knife in as far as it will go and work it back and forth to cut the main arteries. If possible, place carcass on a slant so blood runs away from, not under, the hide.

Place the animal so back legs are lower than the head (hoist off the ground if it is not too heavy), on the under side make a short cut at the base of the first rib, large enough to insert the left hand. Slit with the point of the knife to the vent and around the genital organs and vent. Then start from the middle again and slit forward to the throat. Tie string around rectum and around tube that enters stomach before cutting them off. Remove all viscera and chest organs. Take out heart and liver with care so as not to break the bile sac, which should be removed carefully from the liver. Discard viscera some distance from carcass to avoid attracting flies.

In the dry climate of the Interior, expose meat to the air to form crust that soon hardens enough to keep out flies. Otherwise, tie cheesecloth or rags over the meat to keep out flies, or smear the surface with blood from the body cavity to form a crust that flies cannot penetrate.

Cool meat as rapidly as possible. Cut legs off below knee joint. Remove hide of large animal to hasten cooling and prevent flavor from penetrating the meat. Spread the legs apart, tie them to a gambrell stick, and hoist the carcass several feet off the ground or onto a brush heap.

Cut a large carcass into quarters to hasten cooling and make it easier to carry. Game should not be dragged. If too heavy to carry on a pole, try an Indian travois: Cut two poles twelve feet long with natural bows like sled runners; peel the bowed part and tie upper ends together. Place two crosspieces to form a triangle well to the back to hold the carcass. This improvised sled is surprisingly easy to haul. Do not carry game over the hot engine of the car, exposed to fumes. Better travel at night than expose meat to hot sunlight.

Hang meat to ripen several days in a cool, airy place protected from sun and rain. If unskinned, hang the head up. The natural direction of the hair keeps out rain and snow. A smudge under the meat will help to keep flies away.

When meat has cooled and aged a week or more, cut up the quarters as for beef or lamb – legs for braised steaks or roasts; back for tender steaks, roasts or chops; shoulder, flank, brisket and shanks for stews, soups and ground meat. If animal is very tender, more leg meat may be used for steaks.

Cookery

The same principles apply to the cooking of game as to other meats. Cook tender cuts–sirloin, back, ribs, round and shoulder steaks from young animals–with dry heat; broil, fry, or roast in the oven. Less tender cuts and meat from old animals may be braised or pot-roasted in a covered kettle or pressure cooker with moisture added.

Wild game often lacks fat and needs to be larded. With an ice pick or skewer, insert slivers of salt pork into the lean meat, or grease well with oil or bacon fat.

To tenderize less tender meat, cook it or soak it in weak acids such as tomato juice, sour milk, diluted vinegar or lemon juice.

Use the bony and least-tender cuts for stews and soups. A pressure-cooker cuts cooking time. Always use 10 pounds of pressure for meat, and cook half as long as without pressure.

Wild game flavor increases with aging or ripening. Some permit meat to hang several weeks to ripen. Those who prefer less flavor can reduce or avoid it by the following methods:

Use, freeze, can or brine meat within a week or ten days of kill.

Soak meat overnight in vinegar or baking soda solution, or a mixture of oil and vinegar.

Skim and remove the fat and "fell" which contain most of the "off" flavor. Game meats cooked with beef suet or bacon fat will take on the flavor of beef or bacon fat.

Use seasonings, spices, herbs and sauces liberally.

Reindeer, caribou, moose, buffalo (bison) and deer have somewhat similar characteristics and require similar cooking methods. The cuts resemble beef or lamb cuts and may be substituted for beef or lamb in any recipe.

Camp Meat

Brains, heart, liver, tongue and organ meats are used without ripening. The narrow strip of meat along the backbone may also be used in camp. With the point of the knife rip out the "backstrap" and cut it into 1/4 inch slices. Brush with oil and onion or garlic, place on a green "wiener stick" and roast over hot coals. Season to taste and serve between slices of bread.

University of Alaska Agricultural Extension Service

Roast Venison

5 lb. venison leg roast, boned and tied
Salt, pepper, garlic salt
Shortening, flour

Grease a baking pan. Sprinkle meat with seasoning, rub top with shortening, sprinkle lightly all over with flour.

Place in baking pan and sear at 500° for 15 minutes. Reduce heat to 200° and roast 50 minutes per pound. This will result in rare juicy and tender meat. If you like it well done, roast a little longer increasing heat to 300° for the last hour.

I find that venison is very much like lamb and if the cook follows instructions for cooking lamb, as given in standard cookbooks, she can hardly go wrong.

Moose Rump Roast

With 5 to 5½ lb. rolled moose rump roast, proceed as above until meat has roasted for 5 hours. Then raise heat to 250° for 1½ to 2 hours more of roasting. If meat is seared while still frozen, this time will be sufficient to make it done—barely pink but juicy and tender. If meat is thawed first, roasting time can be shortened somewhat. (I find the slow roasting temperature makes the meat juicy and tender.)

Mamie Jensen, Douglas

Steak Delicious

Take one package Lipton's dry onion soup, pour ½ of package on a good-sized piece of heavy foil, lay unsalted caribou, moose, venison or round steak on top, add rest of soup on top of steak, add 3 tsp. water. Fold foil tightly around so juice can't leak out. Bake in hot coals of campfire 1¼ hours or until done. Test carefully by piercing top of foil with fork or tip of sharp knife. (Diced carrot may be added inside package.)

Isabelle Woolcock, Palmer

Venison and Noodles

2 or 3 lbs. neck meat or 2 to 4 venison shanks. Cover with cold water and boil until tender. Season with salt, pepper and 1 large onion, sliced. Cook until onion is tender. Remove meat, cut into serving portions, and keep hot. Add homemade or packaged noodles to rapidly boiling broth. As soon as noodles are done, add meat, heat if necessary, and serve.

Mamie Jensen, Douglas

Venison Taku

Take a leg or shoulder roast of venison and roast in the usual manner, with your favorite seasoning. When done, remove from pan and keep hot on back of stove.

Pour off top grease in roaster, leaving crusty ingredients and small amount of grease. Add 1 qt. water. Place in oven until water boils. Add 1 package spaghetti or Chinese noodles. Return to oven and stir occasionally until tender. It will turn light chocolate brown and is most delicious served hot with the roast.

Kenneth Junge, Juneau

Steak in a Package

1 cup catsup
¼ cup flour
1 large onion, sliced
Salt and pepper
2 lbs. round steak (moose, caribou, venison, elk) cut 1" thick
2 tbsp. lemon juice or 1 lemon sliced thin

Tear off length of aluminum foil, fold double. Mix catsup and flour and put in center of foil, place steak on it and season. Add remaining catsup mixture and onion slices, sprinkle with lemon juice or top with lemon slices. Fold foil over and seal securely. Place in shallow baking pan and bake in very hot oven (450°) 1½ hours or until done. May also be baked in hot coals of campfire.

Jeanne Woods, Palmer

Pit-Fire Roast Venison

Keep a good fire going in a pit about 1 foot deep until it is full of red coals. Have at least 4 to 6 inches of red coals for your roasting pit. Prepare a game roast of venison or moose with salt, pepper and any other seasoning you desire. Place in heavy foil and seal edges by carefully folding them together. Bank coals around roast, cover all with sand and let roast 6 to 8 hours. Remove sand carefully and use care also in opening the foil. Save the juices to serve over the sliced roast meat.

Mark Jensen, Douglas

Swiss Moose Steak

Prepare 2 or 2½ lbs. moosemeat by cutting into chunks about 1½" thick and 4" square. You can utilize less tender cuts this way. Pound flour and meat tenderizer into it with back of knife or chopper. Brown in Dutch oven, or brown in skillet and transfer to suitable pan. Salt and pepper to taste. Add, in layers with meat, 1 large onion chopped, 2 cans tomato sauce, 1 can mushrooms. Simmer slowly for 1 hour or until meat is fork-tender.

This dish keeps well if you want to prepare it ahead of time and reheat it just before serving.

Lucille Goetz Weir, Douglas

Moose Steak with Dutch Oven Dumplings

Cut 1 lb. moose steak into serving pieces. Season with salt and pepper and fry until very brown on both sides. Cover with boiling water and cook in Dutch oven until tender.

Make dumplings with 1 cup flour, 2 tsp. baking powder, ½ tsp. salt and enough milk to make a very thick dough. (Or use biscuit or pancake mix, following instructions on package.) Drop a spoonful of dough on each piece of meat. Cover with tight lid and cook 15 minutes. Do not lift lid during cooking.

Louise Juhnke, Chugiak

Moose Pot Roast in Barbecue Sauce

4 lb. rump, round or chuck moosemeat
1 cup tomato sauce
½ cup vinegar
3 tsp. salt
¼ tsp. pepper
2 tsp. chili powder
¼ tsp. paprika

Brown meat thoroughly on all sides in a heavy kettle or Dutch oven. Mix together the tomato sauce, vinegar, salt, pepper, chili powder and paprika. Pour over browned meat. Cover and simmer gently over low heat, until tender, about 3 hours. Turn meat several times during cooking and add a little water if necessary to keep meat from sticking. Makes 6 to 8 servings.

If moose lacks fat, add 2 tbsp. salad oil to the tomato sauce mixture. For a thicker gravy, remove meat to a serving platter, mix 1 tbsp. flour and 2 tbsp. water to a smooth paste, and stir into the liquid in the kettle.

Teen Cox, Skagway

Venison Shank with Parsley Dumplings

Season the shank with salt, pepper, celery salt and paprika. Brown in Dutch oven or kettle with tight-fitting lid. When very brown, add 1 cup red wine, cover and simmer until meat is tender. Then add peeled carrots, onions and potatoes and a little water. Let vegetables steam rather than boil, but do not let the meat go dry.

When vegetables are almost done, add 1 or 2 cans cream of mushroom soup, depending upon amount of meat and vegetables used. When this comes to a boil drop in the dumplings (they should rest on vegetables and meat, not in the gravy), dipping the spoon in the gravy first, so dumplings will slip off easily. Cover tightly and cook 15 minutes without lifting cover.

Dumplings may be made from a biscuit mix, adding 1 tsp. sugar, 1 pinch salt and 2 tbsp. dried chopped parsley.

Mrs. Earle L. Hunter, Juneau

Barbecued Venison

(Can be used with the tougher cuts.)

Cut meat in cubes about 1½″ to 2″ square and brown in medium-hot fat. Rendered salt pork is best, with bacon drippings a close second. While venison is browning in a heavy skillet, make sauce as follows:

- ½ cup catsup
- ½ cup wine vinegar
- 2 tbsp. Worcestershire sauce
- ½ tsp. hot sauce
- 2 tbsp. brown sugar
- 1 tsp. salt
- ½ tsp. pepper
- 2 cloves garlic, minced
- Juice of 1 lemon

Put all in saucepan, bring to a boil and simmer for 20 minutes. Add venison and stir to cover all pieces well. In separate saucepan fry very thin slices of onion. Do not chop, but cut these slices in half to have attractive half-rings. Add cooked onions to venison, cook covered about 1 hour or until tender. Watch to be sure the sauce does not cook dry, and add more liquid if necessary. You may serve sauce separately, with potatoes or rice.

Mrs. Dan H. Ralston, Juneau

Sta-fa-ta

(A good way to use tougher portions of moose or caribou).

Cut meat into serving-size pieces, brown in fat or oil, place in kettle and add: 1 or 2 cloves garlic, minced; 1 chopped onion, enough canned tomatoes to just about cover the meat. Season with salt, pepper and a small amount of thyme. Cover and simmer until tender, being sure meat doesn't stick to bottom of kettle. Thicken gravy, if necessary, and serve with rice, noodles or the like.

John Rumohr, by Mommsen, Palmer

Moose Stroganoff

- 3 lbs. lean moose round steak
- 4 tbsp. olive oil or other shortening
- 2 tbsp. flour
- 2 tbsp. salt
- 2 cups mushrooms
- 1 pt. sour cream
- 1 tsp. paprika
- 1 tsp. pepper
- 2 tbsp. butter

Trim fat and gristle from the meat and cut against the grain into strips 1″ long and ¼″ thick. Heat oil in frying pan and cook meat covered, over low flame, turning several times. After 35 minutes or so, add mushrooms and cook 10 minutes more. Add more oil if pan gets too dry. Now put meat and mushrooms in top of double boiler and set aside.

Add butter and flour to juices left in frying pan and smooth this gravy.

Mix in sour cream and let all these juices cook slowly together until they're properly married. Pour this sauce over moosemeat and mushrooms and cook in double boiler 10 minutes. Serve on rice or slices of toast.

This can be made the day before and reheated in double boiler a little while before you're ready to eat.

Mamie Jensen, Douglas

Hunters' Casserole

1 lb. cabbage, shredded fine
1 green pepper
1 onion, medium size, chopped
1 pimento, size of dollar, chopped
1 lb. round steak cut into cubes
½ lb. pork cut into cubes
2 celery stalks, cut fine
Salt and pepper to taste

Steam cabbage, green pepper, onion and pimento a few minutes in a little water. Brown meats in a little butter, stirring so it won't burn. Add a little water, let simmer slowly until tender, add chopped celery.

In greased casserole, alternate layers of meat mixture and cabbage mixture sprinkling with a little flour. Add sliced carrots or potato onto the top, pour on a can of bouillon or consommé, cover and let steam until the top vegetables are done.

Mrs. Arne Shudshift, Douglas

Ragout of Caribou

2 lbs. bottom round of caribou, cut in serving-size pieces and dredged in flour

1 medium onion, chopped
1 garlic clove
1½ tbsp. butter
1 tsp. paprika
Salt and pepper to taste
1 cup celery diced in ½" pieces
2 oz. canned mushroom pieces
14-oz. can tomato sauce
2 tbsp. flour

Sauté onions and garlic in butter until onions are soft and clear. Remove garlic clove. Add meat, paprika, salt and pepper. Cook until meat is browned. Add tomato sauce or juice, cover and simmer gently for 1 hour. Add diced celery, cook 15 minutes more, then add mushrooms. Cover and continue to simmer gently until tender. Sift 2 tbsp. flour into the ragout to thicken sauce. Total cooking time 1½ to 2 hours. Serve with boiled rice, buttered noodles or polenta.

U. of A. AES

Ragout of Beef, Venison or Moose

On 1 lb. cubed stewing meat, sprinkle salt, pepper and flour, and brown in 2 or 3 tbsp. fat in heavy pan. Add 1 small onion, chopped, or dried onion flakes, ¼ cup chopped green pepper, ¾ cup chopped celery or ¼ cup dried celery tops, 2 tsp. chopped or dried parsley. Sprinkle with paprika, add hot water to cover, cook slowly in covered pan 2½ to 3 hours.

To thicken gravy, blend 1 or 2 tbsp. flour with a little water, and stir slowly into stew. Season to taste with salt, pepper, chili powder, chili sauce, catsup or horseradish. Yield: 4 servings.

U. of A. AES

Venisonburger Hot Dish

Place in a flat, greased baking dish: a layer of sliced raw potatoes, seasoned with salt and pepper; a layer of sliced onion; a layer of chopped green pepper.

Fry about 2 slices diced bacon until partly done, sprinkle it and the fat over vegetables, then add a generous layer of seasoned venisonburger.

Dilute 1 can tomato soup with ½ can water and pour over other ingredients; dot with pieces of cheese. Bake 1 to 1½ hours in moderate oven (350°).

Mrs. Mark Jensen, Douglas

Venison Lunch

- 1 lb. ground venison
- 1 onion
- 2 tbsp. catsup
- 2 tsp. prepared mustard
- ½ tsp. salt
- 1 can chicken gumbo soup
- ½ can water

Brown meat and onion in melted fat in a skillet. Add other ingredients and simmer 30 minutes. Serve over boiled rice.

Mrs. Neva Jensen, Douglas

One-Dish Meal for Four

- ½ cup chopped onion
- 1 tsp. garlic powder or 1 small clove garlic
- 2 tsp. salt
- 1 tsp. pepper
- 1 lb. ground venison or moose
- 1 6-oz. can tomato paste
- 1 tsp. Worcestershire sauce
- 1 cup undiluted evaporated milk
- 1 cup canned string beans, drained
- 1 cup uncooked macaroni

Cook macaroni in lightly salted water, drain and blanch. Brown onion, meat and garlic in heavy skillet, add tomato paste, Worcestershire sauce and evaporated milk, then string beans, salt and pepper. Pour meat mixture over cooked macaroni in buttered Dutch oven and put on the fire for 30 minutes. If using a camp stove, bake 30 minutes at 350°.

Thelma Peterson, Elfin Cove

Porcupines (Meatballs)

- 1½ lb. ground moose or caribou
- 1 small onion
- 1 egg (Matanuska fresh)
- ½ cup bread or cracker crumbs
- ½ cup uncooked rice
- Salt and pepper

Mix thoroughly and form into balls. Put into a greased casserole and pour on one can tomato soup or tomato juice with chili powder added. Bake uncovered in moderate oven 1½ hours.

Maud, Palmer

Moose Slumgullion

In large skillet or kettle, brown 1½ to 2 lb. mooseburger and one large minced onion, seasoned with a good-sized slug of garlic salt and enough salt and pepper to suit. When meat is nicely browned, add a No. 2½ can of tomatoes or tomato puree. Simmer about an hour and add one package of previously cooked spaghetti or noodles. Season to taste and serve.

Dana Niemann, Palmer

Picnic Burgers (For Outdoor Grilling)

- 1½ lb. ground moosemeat
- ¾ cup rolled oats, uncooked
- ¼ cup chopped onion
- 2 tsp. salt
- ⅛ tsp. pepper
- 1 cup tomato juice

Mix all ingredients thoroughly and shape into 9 flat circles. Pan-fry only until meat is browned. Chill thoroughly, wrap each in aluminum foil and keep in refrigerator until you leave. Unwrap burgers and grill over the campfire, about 5 minutes on each side. Serve immediately.

Anonymous

Come and Get It!

1 lb. ground venison
1 large onion, chopped
2 slices bacon, diced
1 No. 2½ can tomatoes
¼ cup raw rice
1 small head cabbage
Salt and pepper

Fry the bacon, push aside in the skillet and brown the venison and onion in the fat. When all are nicely browned, add the tomatoes, cabbage shredded as for cole slaw, and uncooked rice. Season to your taste, cover the skillet, set it on the back of the stove and let it simmer for 1 hour. If more liquid is needed to prevent sticking, add a little water.

Mamie Jensen, Douglas

Skillet Meat Loaf

1 lb. ground venison or moose
½ lb. pork sausage
1 egg, slightly beaten
1 medium potato, shredded
1 small onion, chopped
1 tsp. salt
Dash of pepper
¼ tsp. dry sage

Heat 1 tbsp. shortening in heavy skillet with a tight-fitting lid. Form a loaf of the above ingredients, brown it well on both sides and reduce heat to simmer. Dissolve 1 beef bouillon cube in 1½ cup boiling water or use 1½ cup hot venison or moose stock. Add ½ cup of this to meat loaf; cover and simmer for 15 minutes. Turn loaf and add 6 stalks celery, chopped, 6 small carrots cut in half, and remaining cup bouillon. Cover and simmer 30 to 40 minutes or until vegetables are tender. Pour off meat juice, make gravy with it and serve with the loaf. Serves 4 to 6.

Anonymous

German Meatballs

2 cups grated raw potato
2 lb. ground moose
½ lb. ground pork (if you have it)
2 tbsp. grated onion
2 eggs
2 tbsp. lemon juice
2½ tsp. salt
Dash pepper

Mix all ingredients, form into balls, roll in flour, poach in stock (canned consommé, bouillon cubes dissolved in water, or liquor from cooked moose) for 30 minutes; drain and keep warm while you make sauce, as follows:

Blend 4 tbsp. flour and 3 tbsp. butter in pan, add 2 cups stock in which meatballs were cooked, season with salt and pepper, cook until thick. Add 1 tsp. caraway seed and the meatballs. Serve with cooked red cabbage and noodles sprinkled with buttered crumbs.

Anonymous

Mexican Rice with Moose

2 tbsp. fat
1 cup raw rice
1 small onion, minced
½ green pepper, chopped
1 tbsp. salt
2 tsp. chili powder
1 No. 303 can tomatoes
2 cups water
1 lb. ground moose

Wash rice well and dry on paper toweling. Brown onion, rice and meat in fat (add another tbsp. fat if necessary). Add remaining ingredients, mix well and cover. Simmer until rice is done, about 30 minutes. Do not stir after cooking starts, as this breaks the rice grains and mixture tends to become sticky.

Moose Chili Rice

Same as Mexican Rice but substitute 1 can chili con carne without beans for the can of tomatoes.

Lester W. Juhnke, Chugiak

Upside Down Mooseburger Pie

Mince one medium-sized onion and put in heavy skillet with small amount of hot fat. When onion is slightly cooked, add 1 can cream of tomato soup and simmer until onion is tender. Add 1 lb. ground moose and salt and pepper to taste. Continue to simmer, stirring frequently, until meat is cooked thoroughly. Top with baking powder biscuit dough and bake in oven until topping is done. Turn out upside down on platter and serve.

Dana Niemann, Palmer

Easy Tamale Pie

¼ cup butter or shortening
1 lb. ground moose, venison or caribou
1 can tomatoes
1 can cream style corn
1 tsp. cumin (if you have it)
1 cup cornmeal
1 cup milk
2 eggs, beaten
1 tsp. salt
1 tsp. chili powder
1 clove garlic or dash garlic salt or powder

Brown the meat in the shortening. Mix with other ingredients, pour into pan or casserole and bake in moderate oven (350°) for 1½ hours.

Mrs. Mark Jensen, Douglas

Laura's Pizza Pie a la Mooseburger

Make your own favorite baking-powder biscuit dough, roll it thin and line a deep pie pan, crimp the edges and bake until done.

Place butter or drippings in a skillet and heat. Add the following in amounts according to the size of the pie:

1 or 2 lb. ground moose seasoned with Adolph's meat tenderizer
1 medium or large onion, diced
1 chopped green pepper
½ cup chopped celery, if desired

Brown lightly and cook until done.

Over biscuit-dough pie shell spread 1 small can tomato paste, 1 small can tomato sauce and the meat and vegetables. On top put thin wedges of sharp cheese and put in oven long enough to melt cheese. Serve piping hot.

Laura Mommsen, Palmer

SITKA BLACKTAIL DEER

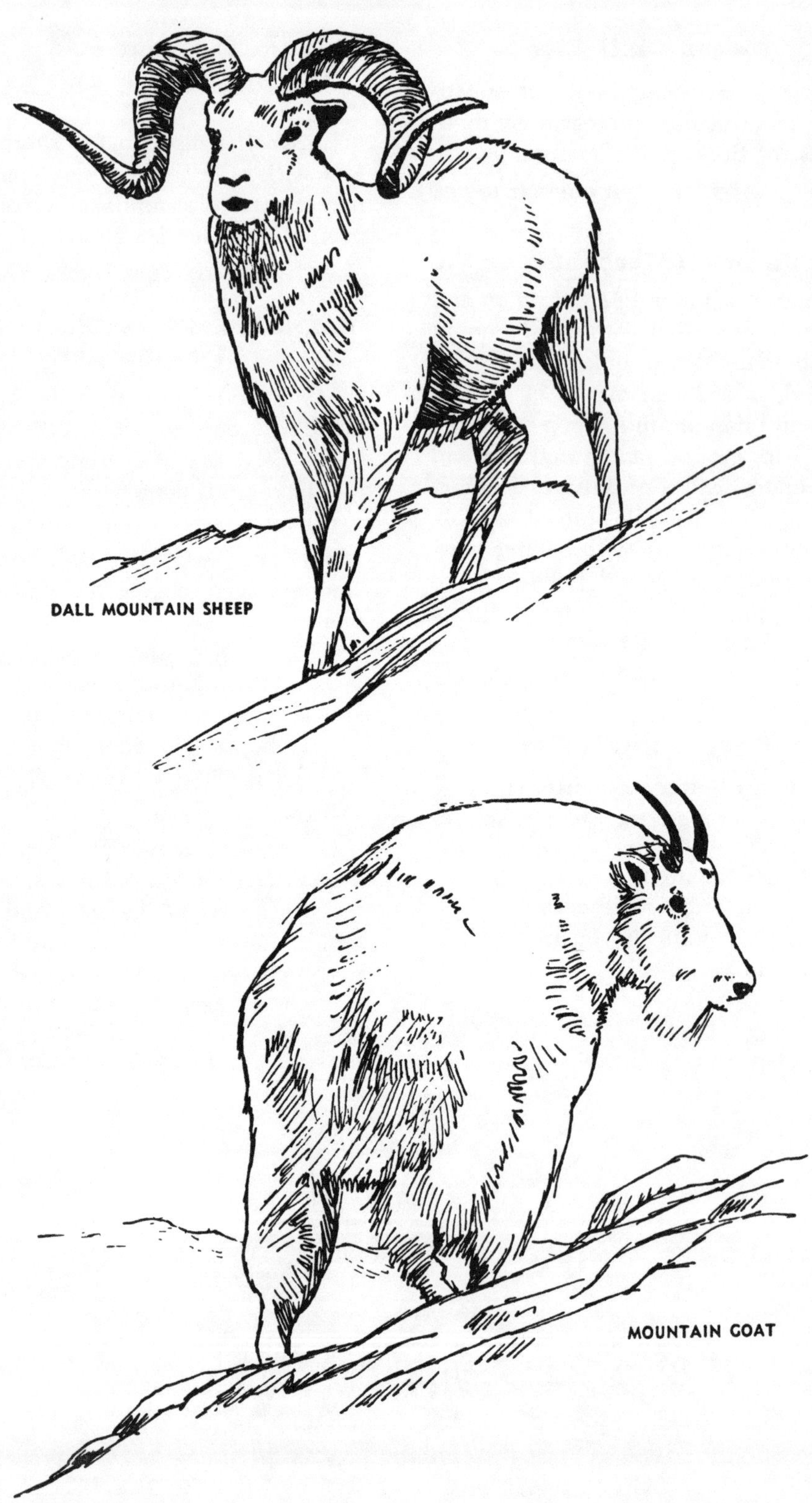
DALL MOUNTAIN SHEEP
MOUNTAIN GOAT

Chapter **3**

MOUNTAIN SHEEP AND GOAT

Mountain (Dall) Sheep

Sheep meat is best not kept too long in the freezer. If meat has been stored one to two months, the tallow should be trimmed as close as possible as it absorbs odors and will taste rancid.

Sheep can be cooked the same as beef, broiled, fried, roasted or stewed. It is a flavorful meat and does not need heavy seasonings.

Harold Curtis, Anchorage

Stuffed Sheep Shoulder

4 pounds shoulder roast
1 cup rice
2 tbsp. fat
2 bay leaves
1 onion, chopped
1 green pepper, chopped
1½ cups quartered (or canned) tomatoes
1 tsp. salt

Bone shoulder to make pocket for stuffing. Cook rice in boiling salted water. Drain. Melt fat in heavy pan or skillet, add bay leaves (crushed), chopped onion and green pepper. Cook slowly until tender. Add tomatoes and salt, cook five minutes more, then mix in rice with a fork. Fill pocket in meat with rice mixture, fasten with skewers, place on rack fat side up and roast in a slow oven (325°) for 2½ hours. Do not cover.

Anonymous, Birchwood

Shepherd's Pie, with Sheep or Goat

Chop leftover meat into cubes and moisten with leftover gravy, adding a bit of chopped onion if desired. Place in greased casserole and dot with butter or bacon drippings. Cover with hot mashed potatoes (can use packaged instant potatoes) and spread top with beaten egg yolk mixed with 2 tsp. cold water. Bake in hot oven (400° F.) until nicely browned, about 20 minutes.

Anonymous, Anchorage

Sheep Roast

Roll sheep roast in flour. Season with salt and pepper, and garlic salt if desired. Brown in hot fat on top of stove. When nicely browned on all surfaces, place roaster in oven and cover. Roast at 300° F. allowing cooking time as for rare, medium or well-done beef. Remove cover for last 30 minutes of roasting if desired. Or cook in Dutch oven, same as any roast.

Aileen Curtis, Anchorage

Broiled Dall Chops

Cut ribs into chops 1 inch thick. Slash fat to prevent curling. Place on grate or rack about three inches above hot coals of campfire. Brush chops with French dressing and salt and pepper to taste. Broil 7 minutes on each side, 14 minutes in all.

Anonymous, Birchwood

Sheepburgers

1 pound ground sheep meat
½ tbsp. fat
4 slices diced bacon
1 tsp. salt

Heat fat in heavy skillet. Add diced bacon and salt to meat and mix well. Add pepper if desired. Shape into patties not more than ½ inch thick and pan-fry in hot fat until well browned on both sides. Serve very hot.

Anonymous, Birchwood

Sheep or Goat Stew

2 pounds meat
1 tbsp. fat
1 qt. water
½ cup pearl barley
½ cup old-fashioned oatmeal
1 sliced onion
2 tbsp. chopped parsley
3 tbsp. chopped celery leaves
6 medium potatoes
2 tsp. salt

Heat fat in heavy kettle. Cut meat into 2-inch cubes and brown well in hot fat. Add water, barley, onion, parsley, celery and salt. Cook slowly 1½ hours. Add potatoes and oatmeal and continue cooking until potatoes are tender. Serve with crackers and cheese. Serves 6 to 8.

Louise Juhnke, Chugiak

Sheep or Goat Rib Barbecue

(Saves carrying out the ribs, and is an excellent camp meal.) Clean rib cage, which has been separated into two sides. Salt and pepper, how much you like. Prop one on each side of a bed of hot coals. Keep turning until cooked through and very nicely browned. Then have at them. Good!

Buck Moore, Anchorage

Sheep Skillet

1½ pounds sheep meat cut into 2-inch pieces
2 tbsp. fat
Flour
1 tbsp. Worcestershire sauce
1 tsp. salt
1 cup tomato juice

Roll sheep chunks in flour and brown in hot fat. When browned on all sides, add Worcestershire sauce, salt and tomato juice. Cover and cook slowly until meat is tender, 1½ to 2 hours. Serve over boiled or steamed rice.

Louise Juhnke, Chugiak

Goat or Sheep Stew

Cut 3 pounds goat or sheep forequarter into 2-inch cubes, place in kettle, cover with boiling water and cook slowly until tender, about 1½ hours. Add:

1 cup cubed carrots
1 cup cubed turnips
3 cups cubed potatoes

1 tsp. salt
Pepper to taste
1 sliced onion (medium)

Cook until vegetables are done. Thicken with flour mixed with a little water, if desired.

Anonymous, Anchorage

Roast Mountain Goat

5 to 6 pound roast
1 or 2 cloves garlic
Salt and pepper

Clean meat thoroughly. Make openings all over and insert tiny slivers of garlic. Salt and pepper entire surface. Put small amount of water in roasting pan and put roast in it. Roast in slow oven (325°) until tender, then increase heat to 400° for quick browning.

Anonymous, Anchorage

BROWN BEAR
BLACK BEAR

Chapter 4

BEAR

Bear meat must be cooked until well done, as it is subject to trichinae contamination the same as pork. Thorough cooking kills trichinae and makes the meat safe for consumption.

Bear meat is high in fat, which can be rendered and used the same as lard. Keep it tightly sealed in a cool, dark place and use it for deep-fat frying, for pastry, cakes and so forth.

Bear Steaks or Chops

Cut steaks or chops 1 inch thick into serving-size pieces. Mix ½ cup flour, ½ tsp. cloves and 1 tsp. ginger, and pound into the meat on both sides. Brown in fat in a moderately hot skillet, then salt and pepper to taste. Cover skillet and simmer 10 to 15 minutes.

Grace Hanson, Anchorage

Roast Bear

Use about an 8-pound roast off the rump of a young bear. Cover with cold water, add 3 or 4 medium-sized sliced onions, and let soak about 4 hours. Remove from water and wipe dry. Cut 1 small clove garlic into small pieces and, using a sharp knife to make holes, force garlic deep into the meat. Get garlic as near the bone as possible. Season with salt and pepper. Brown in hot bacon drippings. Bake in open pan for 3 hours at 350°, turning the meat several times while cooking.

Guide Ralph Hall
PTA COOKBOOK, Petersburg

Barbecued Bear

This is for a young black bear. If you've got a brownie or a big old black, admire your trophy but open a can of beans when chow time comes!

Sauce

¼ cup vinegar
½ cup water
2 tbsp. sugar
1 tsp. dry mustard
½ tsp. pepper
1½ tsp. salt
¼ tsp. garlic powder
1 tbsp. lemon juice
1 onion, minced
¼ cup salad oil

POLAR BEAR
GRIZZLY BEAR

1 tsp. chili powder
5 squirts tabasco sauce
½ cup catsup
2 tbsp. Worcestershire sauce

Mix all except catsup and Worcestershire sauce. If you have a blender, blend them in it briefly. Simmer 20 minutes, uncovered. Add catsup and Worcestershire sauce and bring to a boil. Remove from heat.

Meanwhile, place roasting-size piece of bear meat in 325° oven. When well glazed, baste with sauce. Continue roasting, basting frequently, 3 to 4 hours or until fork-tender. Time of course depends upon size of roast and age of animal.

Serve with baked potatoes, corn-on-the-cob and crisp salad.

Mrs. Sam H. Roberson, Douglas

Sieg's Barbecue Sauce for Bear or Moose

1½ cup hot water
1 tsp. prepared mustard
1 cup tomato sauce or ½ cup catsup
¼ tsp. tabasco sauce
Juice of 1 lemon
1 tsp. grated lemon rind
1 tbsp. Worcestershire sauce
1 medium onion, minced
1 clove garlic, chopped fine
3 bay leaves
½ cup chopped celery
¼ tsp. thyme

Mix ingredients. Cover and cook very slowly for 2 or 3 hours. Add more water if needed.

Dr. W. G. Sieg, Haines

Chapter 5

RABBIT OR HARE

Extreme care should be taken in preparing rabbit because of the possibility of tularemia (rabbit fever). A rabbit that is slow to move or looks sick should be discarded. Care should be taken in handling rabbits, as some illnesses have been contracted from infected rabbits through injuries on the hands. Rabbit should always be cooked until well done.

Baked Rabbit

1 wild rabbit
Salt and pepper
Bacon drippings
Flour
Your favorite bread or potato stuffing

Clean and dress rabbit, disjoint, and wash in strong salt water. Dry. Season with salt and pepper and roll in flour. Brown on all sides in hot bacon drippings. Cover tightly and remove from heat. Prepare stuffing and place it in well-greased Dutch oven. Lay browned pieces of rabbit over the stuffing, cover, place on a light bed of coals and rake hot coals over Dutch oven, covering it completely. This should cook from the top down. Cook until rabbit is tender and stuffing is done. If cooking in an oven, bake about 1 hour at 350°. Add more water if stuffing appears to be getting dry.

Hare and Onions

1 wild hare or rabbit
Bacon grease
Flour
Salt and pepper
Dry onions, sliced thin
½ to 1 cup water

Dress and disjoint hare, wash thoroughly in salted water, dry, season with salt and black pepper to taste and roll in flour. Brown in hot bacon grease, turning often. When nicely browned on all sides add sliced onions, the amount depending entirely upon how many you're serving and how well they like onions. Pour on the water, cover tightly, and proceed as with chicken.

Louise Juhnke, Chugiak

Roast Rabbit

Make dressing with 1 pint mashed potatoes, 2 tbsp. butter or margarine, 1 tsp. salt, ½ tsp. pepper, 1½ tsp. thyme or 1 tsp. sage, 1 cup chopped celery or 1½ tsp. celery salt. (If using celery salt, cut down on the table salt.)

Dress and wash one rabbit, fill the body with stuffing and skewer. Place in baking pan with legs folded under body and skewer in this position. Strip back of rabbit with bacon or pork to keep it from drying out. Roast in 400° oven for ten minutes, then pour on 1 or 2 cups hot water and cook 35 to 45 minutes. Shortly before the end of cooking time, take off the bacon and let the rabbit brown.

This recipe can be used with Dutch oven and campfire. Just cover the Dutch oven with coals and allow a little more cooking time.

Pan-Fried Rabbit

Disjoint rabbit, wipe clean, and parboil 10 minutes in water to which 1 tsp. soda has been added. Drain. Season with salt and pepper. Dip in beaten egg and roll in bread crumbs. Fry in hot fat—hot enough to brown a bread cube in sixty seconds. Drain off all fat. One good way to remove fat is to hold each piece over flame on long-handled fork.

Rabbit may be prepared this way for deep-fat frying.

Alma Haik, Anchorage

Yummy Rabbit

1 young rabbit
1½ tbsp. bacon drippings
1 cup boiling water
1 beef or chicken bouillon cube
¼ cup lemon juice (may be canned)
¾ cup orange juice (may be canned)
Small can mushrooms
Green pepper
Parsley
Pinch of ginger

Disjoint rabbit and brown in fat. Dissolve bouillon cube in water and add it and other ingredients. Cover and cook slowly until tender.

Vernon Haik, Anchorage

PORCUPINE
BEAVER
MUSKRAT

Chapter **6**

BEAVER AND MUSKRAT

These animals are herbivorous and the flesh is sweet and palatable.

A dressed muskrat weighs about a pound and makes 2 servings. The meat is dark, fine-grained, and has a distinctive, gamy flavor. It can be roasted, broiled, braised or stewed.

Alice Hanson, Anchorage

Roast Beaver

Remove all the fat you can from the beaver, as the fat is what gives it a strong taste. Using 1 tsp. soda to 1 qt. water, parboil beaver for 10 to 15 minutes. Drain and dry, season with salt and pepper, add onion, sliced, and roast in 350° oven until well done.

Anonymous, Anchorage

Pan-Fried Beaver

Disjoint beaver as you would a chicken and remove all fat. Parboil 10 minutes in soda-water (1 tsp. baking soda to 1 qt. water), drain and rinse. Cook in fresh water with small chunks of bacon until beaver is tender. Drain again, season with salt, pepper, and thyme, paprika or sage, then brown in hot bacon drippings.

Use only young beaver in this recipe, as large ones have a tendency to toughen.

Vernon Haik, Anchorage

Beaver or muskrat may be used with Alma Haik's Roast Rabbit recipe, above. Be sure to soak the meat overnight, using 1 tbsp. salt to 1 qt. water, and parboil 20 minutes using 1 tsp. salt per qt. water. Then proceed with Roast Rabbit recipe.

Chicken-Fried Muskrat

Soak muskrat overnight in salt water (1 tbsp. per qt.), drain, disjoint and cut into serving pieces. Season with salt, pepper and paprika to taste, then roll in flour and fry in bacon fat until browned on all sides. Cover with sliced onions, salt lightly and pour on 1 cup sour cream. (Condensed milk or reconstituted dried milk may be soured with 2 tsp. vinegar per cup and used in place of sour cream.) Cover tightly and simmer or bake in Dutch oven for one hour.

Vernon Haik, Anchorage

Muskrat

1 muskrat
1 egg, beaten
½ cup milk
1 tsp. salt
½ cup flour
Pepper
Bacon fat

Soak muskrat overnight in salt water (1 tbsp. to 1 qt.), drain, cut into serving-size pieces, parboil in salt water (1 tsp. to 1 qt.) 20 minutes, drain and wipe dry. Make batter of egg, milk, salt, pepper and flour. Dip meat into batter and brown in hot fat. When all pieces are nicely browned, cover and cook over low heat for 1½ hours. Or cook in Dutch oven.

Anonymous, Anchorage

Muskrat

Proceed as above until meat is browned in hot fat. Then put in pan and cover with 1 can tomato sauce, and 1 tsp. Worcestershire sauce or 1 sliced onion or 1 small clove garlic. Cover with 1 cup water and a tight lid and simmer until done, about 1 hour, adding water if needed.

Louise Juhnke, Chugiak

Porcupine

Traditionally, in Alaska, the porcupine is out of season except to the desperate—the lost, injured and hungry—the prospector who has broken through the ice and escaped with only his life, the dog-team mail carrier long delayed by a blizzard, the hunter or fisherman who has barely made it to shore from an overturned boat, the downed bush pilot—because the porcupine, too slow-moving to escape, can be killed with a rock or a stick and its meat could renew a man's chance for survival.

At such times a man isn't going to be fussy about how he cooks a porcupine. He may even eat it raw.

But if a porcupine is making a nuisance of itself around camp, you may need to kill it, and its meat is well worth utilizing. Here's one big-game guide's recipe:

Porcupine Fricassee

Use porcupine legs only, and trim away all fat. Soak in cold, salted water 6 to 10 hours or overnight. Drain. Roll in flour and brown in hot fat. Put it in a Dutch oven. Make gravy with flour, water and the drippings from the fry pan and pour it over the meat. Simmer slowly for about three hours. Season well with salt, pepper and garlic, onions or other herbs.

Mark Jensen, Douglas

CUTTING ANIMAL FOR ORGANS

Chapter 7

ORGAN AND SCRAP MEATS

Moose Heart, Fried

1 moose heart
Fat
Flour, seasoned with salt, pepper and paprika

Trim blood vessels and fat from heart. Wash thoroughly, running cool water over and through heart. Trim out cords. Wipe dry. Slice in ¼-inch-thick slices. Roll in seasoned flour, then brown on both sides in hot fat. Add just enough hot water to cover slices, put on lid and simmer 20 to 30 minutes.

Anonymous, Anchorage

Stuffed Heart

Moose, caribou, venison or beef heart
Bread stuffing
Flour
Fat
Salt
Pepper
Paprika

Trim heart, wash, wipe dry, then fill cavity with favorite bread stuffing. Fasten firmly with skewers and string. Roll in flour that has been seasoned with salt, pepper and paprika. Coat it well, then brown in hot fat. Add ½ cup hot water for one heart, ¼ cup for each additional heart. Cover and simmer until tender, or bake in a moderate oven about 2¼ hours.

Anonymous, Anchorage

Baked Heart

Clean and wash a deer or moose heart. Remove tubes, membranes and fat. Soak in salt water 3 hours. Dry on paper towels. Roll whole deer heart, or moose heart cut into 4 or 6 pieces, in flour and brown in bacon fat. Keep warm on top of stove while you brown salt pork or diced bacon. To drippings add 2 cups diced onions, 1 cup crumbs (cornbread, bread or biscuit), pinch of sage, salt and pepper. Stuff the hearts with the bacon-crumb-onion mixture. Bake in Dutch oven or kettle with a tight lid, in slow oven until done, about 3 hours.

Mrs. E. E. Weschenfelder, Fritz Cove

Venison, Moose, Caribou or Sheep Heart

Wash hearts thoroughly in salt water, removing blood. Put in kettle and pour on boiling water to cover. Add 1 tsp. salt to 1 qt. water, dash of pepper, 1 bay leaf, 1 stalk celery cut in thirds, 1 small carrot, 1 quartered onion. Bring to a boil, then let simmer until meat is tender. Venison hearts take an hour, others a little longer. Test with a fork. Meat can be cooled in broth, then removed and sliced thin for sandwiches. When broth is cold, remove and discard hardened fat. Strain the broth and use it as the base for hearty soups or gravies, or in recipes that call for bouillon.

Mark Jensen, Douglas

Fried Deer Liver and Heart

Soak the liver and heart in salted water overnight. Rinse in fresh water and slice. Season with salt and pepper and fry to a nice brown on both sides. The heart has the texture of liver when fried.

John Hagmeier Sr., Auke Bay

Cow Camp Stew

This dish originated along with the necessity of usurping edible organ meats when a beef was taken for food. The same situation often prevails in the hunting camp. You'll need 1 Dutch oven, 1 cast-iron frying pan and 1 paper sack. Ingredients and proportions vary with the supply on hand. Methods of preparing vary with the location and the individual, as do names for the concoction, the latter being handed down mostly by word of mouth. Some of the names wouldn't look so good in print.

Dice heart and liver in ¾ inch chunks, but keep separate. Put some water in a Dutch oven and keep it hot. Put fat in a skillet and bring it to a smoking heat. Put about 1 cup flour and some salt and pepper into the paper sack, put in chunks of heart and shake well, then put heart into hot fat and fry for 30 minutes, stirring occasionally. Transfer heart to Dutch oven and add potatoes and onions, cut up as desired, add water to cover, put on the lid and bake in oven one hour. Give liver the same treatment but fry it only 10 minutes and add it to the Dutch oven 20 minutes before serving.

One variation is to prepare biscuit dough and lop over the top of the stew after adding liver.

The "ultimate" in the Cow Camp Stew also contains the sweetbreads and "marrow gut," the latter at their best only in an animal under 2 years old.

G. S. "Bud" Mortensen, Petersburg

How to Prepare Wild Game Liver

Soak liver for 2 hours in 1 qt. water to which 3 tbsp. vinegar have been added. Remove from water and wipe dry. Slice not too thin, cutting away gristle and skin, pour boiling water over the slices, stir around for a minute or two until liver looks grayish, chill in cold water, dry on paper towel.

Fried Liver

Dip liver slices (prepared as above) in seasoned flour and fry quickly in bacon fat, turning as soon as the blood starts to show on the top of slice. Turn only once. Do not fry liver too hard, as this makes it dry and unpalatable. Good served with cornbread.

Liver Patties

1 lb. liver (prepared as above)
2 slices bacon
Salt and pepper
1 egg
2 tsp. flour
2 tsp. chopped onion

Grind or chop liver, dice bacon and onion, mix together in a bowl, add the egg, salt and pepper. Shape into small cakes, roll lightly in flour, fry in bacon fat. Serve with cornmeal hot cakes.

Baked Deer or Moose Liver

Soak liver as instructed above, cut away gristle and skin, put strips of bacon or salt pork on top and secure with toothpicks or thin wood strips. Put in a baking dish. Season with 1 bay leaf, 2 whole cloves, 6 peppercorns, 1 carrot and 1 large onion, diced, and chopped celery leaves if you have any. Add 2 cups water or diluted consommé. Cover tightly and bake in a slow oven 2 hours. Cut liver in slices to serve. Make pan gravy and serve over liver slices, with baked potatoes and salad.

Liver Dumplings

1 lb. liver (prepared as above)
1½ tbsp. deer suet
Salt and pepper to taste
1 small onion
Flour
⅛ tsp. nutmeg (if you like)
2 eggs
3 slices dry bread
1 tsp. chopped parsley (if you have)

Chop or grind liver, bacon and suet, add salt and pepper. Soak bread in a little water, squeeze dry and add to liver along with eggs, parsley and seasonings. Add enough flour to bind, drop on top of stew or soup with teaspoon, boil gently for 10 minutes. Very good.

Mrs. E. E. Weschenfelder, Fritz Cove

Broiled Moose Liver

We prefer to soak the liver for ½ hour in cold water to remove some of the blood, then cut it into slices ½ inch thick, place on a rack over the coals and brush with fat, season with salt and pepper, and broil about 15 to 20 minutes on each side. After turning the liver we sometimes add bacon strips and broil three minutes on each side. Be sure to keep liver at least three inches from heat of medium-hot coals.

Chili Liver

After soaking liver and slicing it, dip it in four tbsp. flour that has been seasoned with 1 tsp. dry mustard and ¼ tsp. chili powder and salt and pepper to taste. Then fry in hot fat until done.

Liver Alaska

Soak and slice 1 lb. liver (moose, caribou or what-have-you) and sprinkle with seasoned flour. Saute 2 medium-sized onions and 1 green pepper, sliced, in ¼ cup fat until tender. Remove onion and pepper and brown liver slices in same skillet. Add onion, pepper, 1 can tomato sauce, 1 cup water, and salt and pepper to taste. Cover and simmer 15 minutes; uncover and cook a few minutes longer to thicken sauce. Serve over boiled rice. Makes four to six servings.

Anonymous, Anchorage

Liver in Onions

½ lb. liver
1 cup chopped celery

6 medium onions
10 slices bacon
½ tsp. salt

Pour boiling water over liver and leave it for 2 minutes. Pour off water, remove the thin skin and chop fine. Dice the bacon and fry until crisp. Remove outer skin of onions and as much of the inside as you can, leaving a firm shell. Chop the onion centers, mix with the bacon, liver, celery and salt, and stuff the hollowed-out onions with this mixture. Place in a Dutch oven, sprinkle cracker or bread crumbs over tops, cover oven and put it on the coals, heaping coals up around the lid. Cook 1 hour. Venison, moose or seal liver may be used in this recipe.

Hazel Wimer, Elfin Cove

Crispy Moose Liver

1 lb. liver
1 fresh egg
1 tbsp. water
1 tbsp. lemon juice
1 tsp. salt
¾ cup fine cracker crumbs
2 tbsp. bacon drippings

Beat egg and blend with water, lemon juice and salt. Dip slices of liver in crumbs, then in egg mixture and dip again in crumbs. Brown for 5 minutes on each side. Serve with cranberry or tomato catsup.

(The secret of crispy liver is to dip *fresh* liver in cracker crumbs instead of flour before frying.)

Gussie and Bill Byington, Juneau

Liver Patties

Use enough liver for your party. Chop it and run it through a coarse meat grinder, add finely chopped onion, salt and pepper—how much you like. Shape into patties and fry over slow heat. Never use a hot pan or heat to fry liver, and do not overcook it.

Frank "Buck" Moore, Anchorage

Liver Sausage

For 10 lbs. sausage, use 8 to 8½ lbs. scrap meat and liver.

Cook scrap meat until it can be removed from any bone present, but not until too tender. Cut blood vessels from liver and cut in 4- to 6-inch strips. Cut crosswise through strips with knife so they can be thoroughly scalded, and put in scalding water for 10 to 15 minutes. Grind meat and liver with ¼-inch plate. Add enough of the meat liquor to make the texture soft but not wet.

Add 4 ounces smoked salt, ½ ounce black pepper, 1 tsp. red pepper, 1 tsp. sage, 1 tsp. allspice.

Mix well, stuff into casings and simmer in hot water until the sausage floats, 20 to 30 minutes. Plunge into cold water and chill thoroughly. Drain, wrap in foil or coat with wax, and freeze.

Bertha Meier, Anchorage

Seal Liver Loaf

¼ lb. salt pork
1 lb. seal liver (soaked overnight in salt water)
1½ cup hot water
1 cup cracker crumbs
2 eggs, beaten
1 tbsp. minced onion
1 tsp. poultry seasoning
Salt and pepper to taste

Fry pork, remove from pan, add liver and brown on both sides in the pork fat. Put pork and liver through food chopper, using coarse blade. Pour water over cracker crumbs;

combine meat, crumbs, eggs, onions and seasonings. Place in greased baking dish and bake in moderate oven (375°) 40 minutes. Serve hot or cold. Serves 6. (Other liver may be used in this recipe.)

Teen Cox, Skagway

Tongue

To cook a fresh tongue, wash thoroughly, cover with cold water, add 1 tbsp. salt, 1 small onion, dash of pepper, and 1 bay leaf if desired. Quantities are for a large tongue, as of moose. Cook slowly until tender, 1½ hours per pound. Allow to cool, remove skin, bones and any tissue before tongue becomes too cool. Slice and serve hot or cold.

Anonymous, Anchorage

Deer or Moose Tongue

Soak tongues in salt water and scrub clean. Put in big kettle with a carrot, an onion, and some celery if available. Add salt and pepper, 1 bay leaf, and 2 tbsp. vinegar, cover with boiling water and let simmer for 2 or 3 hours until nice and tender. Take out the tongues, peel off the skin, cut off root ends, and put back in kettle to keep hot.

Serve with horseradish sauce made as follows:

- 3 tbsp. bacon fat
- 3 tbsp. flour
- Salt and pepper
- 2 cups strained broth (from cooking tongues)
- ½ bottle prepared horseradish

Brown the flour in the hot bacon fat, stir in the broth and blend till smooth, add salt and pepper and the horseradish.

Pickled Tongue

- 4 or 6 deer tongues
- Salt
- Mixed spices

Wash deer tongues in salt water, add mixed spices and salt, and simmer gently until done. Cool, peel off skin and cut off root ends. Put in a jar and add the following pickle solution:

- 1 pint vinegar
- 1 pint water
- 1 tbsp. mustard seed
- ½ tsp. mace
- 1 tsp. whole cloves
- 1 tsp. whole allspice
- 1 tsp. peppercorns
- Salt to taste

Boil all this together for 10 minutes, pour over the tongues and let stand for a week. Good sliced for lunches.

(This pickling solution is good for trout, too. Salt the trout overnight, parboil, then let them stand in the solution for a few days. Delicious served cold.)

Mrs. E. E. Weschenfelder, Fritz Cove

Moose Bologna Sausage (Italian Type)

- 15 pounds moose meat with suet
- 2 ounces salt
- 1 cup smoked salt
- 1 ounce black pepper
- 1 ounce coriander
- ¼ ounce mace

Grind meat, add spices and mix with the hands for at least 15 minutes. A small amount of water may be added to make mixing easier. Pack in a pan and let sit in refrigerator overnight. Grind through smaller plate of grinder once or twice. Stuff into casings. If commercial casings are not available, sew sugar sacks into 3-inch tubes. Boil in plain water until the sausage floats.

Moose Sausage (Plain)

15 pounds moose meat with suet
2 ounces sausage seasoning
5 tsp. salt
2 heaping tsp. sage (if desired)
6 chili peppers, crumbled

Grind the meat through coarse grinder, mix in seasonings, let sit in refrigerator overnight, grind through finer plate once. Stuff into casings or pack into plastic bags and freeze.

I use smoke salt for these two sausages and the Liver Sausage, above, to get the smoke taste. I've tried smoking them in the smokehouse for 2 hours, which cuts down the cooking time but makes no difference in flavor or texture.

Bertha Meier, Anchorage

Rullepolse (Meat Roll)

Flank of deer, moose or caribou
Scraps of meat and fat (we use very little tallow)
Seasonings (salt, pepper, chopped onion, ginger, to taste)

Remove bones from flank. Cut scraps into strips, season, spread on flank (small flanks should be sewed together for larger roll), roll and wrap tightly with twine. Keep in the following brine solution until ready to use:

Boil enough water to cover the meat, add enough salt to float a peeled raw potato, boil until salt is dissolved. Add saltpeter (1 tbsp. to 2 gallons of brine) to preserve the color of the meat. Cool the brine and add the meat roll, putting a weight on top to keep roll under brine.

To use, remove from brine (soak overnight in cold water if roll is too salty), boil in fresh water for 2 hours, remove from water and place in a loaf pan with a weight on top to shape it into a firm loaf. When cold, slice it thin and serve. Makes good sandwich meat.

Mrs. Berger Wasvick, from Mrs. Joseph O. Rude, Juneau

Jellied Moose Nose

Cut upper jawbone of moose just below the eyes. Put in large kettle of scalding water and parboil 45 minutes. Remove and cool in cold water. Pick off the hairs as you would feathers from a duck (the boiling loosens them), and wash thoroughly.

Put moose nose in fresh water with onion, a little garlic and pickling spices. Boil gently until tender. Cool overnight in same juice.

In the morning, remove bone and cartilage. The bulb of the nose is white meat, the thin strips along the bone and jowls dark. Slice the meat thin, pack in jars or cans, and cover with the juice. This jells, and when chilled it can be sliced. Serve cold.

The meat of the nose may be pickled in vinegar if desired.

Bertha Meier, Anchorage

Chapter 8

FISH

Oven-Fried Fillets

2 lbs. fillets
1 tbsp. salt
1 cup milk or buttermilk
1 cup browned breadcrumbs, cornmeal or crushed cornflakes
4 tbsp. melted butter or other fat

Cut fillets into serving-size portions. Add salt to milk in shallow pan. Dip fish in milk, roll in crumbs, place in well-greased pan, pour on melted fat. Place pan on rack near top of oven and bake at 500° for 10 to 15 minutes, until fish flakes easily when tested with a fork. Serve immediately on hot platter, plain or with a sauce. Serves 6.

Thelma Rose Lind, Ketchikan
U.S. FWS Home Economist

This recipe, a variation of the Spencer Hot Oven Method, is also excellent for steaks, or any fish cut not more than 1½ inches thick. The quick cooking at high heat retains the moisture and flavor lost in slower pan-frying or baking methods. Less fat may be used, especially when cooking salmon, sablefish or other rich varieties. Greased foil under the fish, turned up slightly at the edges, saves soaking and scrubbing the pan. Lemon, the traditional garnish, should be cut in wedges instead of slices. You can squeeze the juice out of a lemon wedge.

Tartar Sauce

1 cup mayonnaise
2 tsp. lemon juice
1 tbsp. each, minced pickles, parsley, onion and (optional) capers

Mix, and the sauce is ready to serve

Thelma Rose Lind, Ketchikan

Baked Fish Halibut, Salmon or Large Trout

First fillet the fish and cut in serving-size pieces. Place flesh-side up in flat, buttered pan. Sprinkle with salt, pepper, chopped onion and thin slices of lemon. Barely cover with water. Bake in moderate oven for 45 minutes.

While fish is baking, place butter in

RED SALMON (SOCKEYE)

CHUM (DOG) SALMON

PINK (HUMPBACK) SALMON

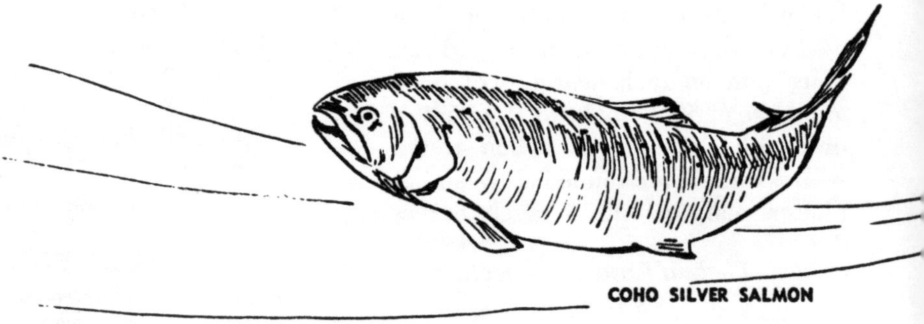

COHO SILVER SALMON

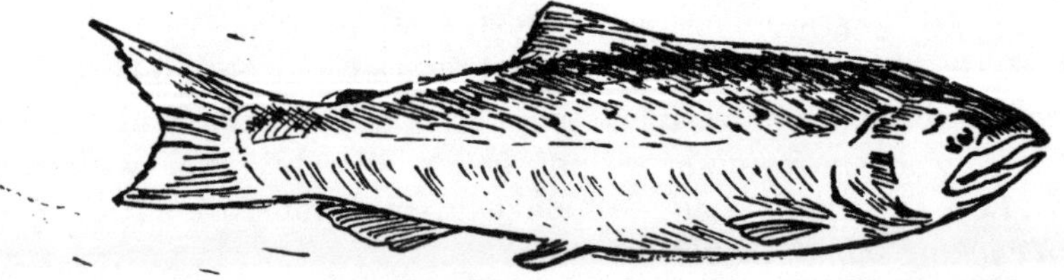

KING SALMON

top of double boiler and stir in enough flour to make a paste. Pour in liquid from baked fish and stir till well cooked. Add canned milk to build ¼ more in volume. Season to taste, pour over fish, sprinkle with grated cheese and parsley flakes and re-heat in the oven.

G. S. "Bud" Mortensen, Petersburg

Scalloped Fish

2 cups cooked fish, any variety
2 tbsp. grated onion
2 cups whitesauce
1 tsp. salt
¼ tsp. pepper
1 cup breadcrumbs
2 tbsp. butter

Remove skin and bones of fish and flake. Into a buttered baking dish place, in layers, 1/3 of the fish, 1/3 of the seasonings and 1/3 of the sauce. Repeat twice. Sprinkle buttered crumbs on top and bake at 350° for 30 minutes.

Jeanne Woods, Palmer

Fish Bowl

1 medium onion
1 medium potato
1 stalk celery
1 large carrot
1 small rutabaga (if you have and if you like)
1 small bay leaf or ¼ tsp. powdered bay leaf
½ tsp. salt
Dash of pepper
1 rounded tbsp. cornstarch dissolved in 1 tbsp. cold water
Fish*

Cut peeled vegetables into bite-size pieces, put vegetables and seasonings in 1 qt. boiling water and cook gently until done. Add fish. Just before serving add butter, a little chopped parsley if you have it, and cornstarch thickening. Serve in bowls and eat with a spoon. Plenty for 2.

*If you use raw fish, cut it into bite-size pieces and add to vegetables after they have cooked a little, and add another ½ tsp. salt.

If you use cooked halibut or salmon, flake it and add at the last, just in time to get it heated through but not recooked. Any liquid from the fish should be added as soon as possible to flavor the vegetables.

If you use canned Norwegian fish balls, pour the liquid into the cooking vegetables and add the balls at the last.

1 cup of fish is enough. More may be used.

Mamie Jensen, Douglas

Fiskesalat

Any variety cold, cooked fish
Lettuce
1 egg yolk, beaten
¼ tsp. salt
4 tbsp. cream
½ tsp. mustard
Pepper, parsley, vinegar

Make a dressing of the egg yolk, cream, vinegar, seasonings and spices. Put lettuce and fish in a salad bowl, pour on dressing and sprinkle with parsley.

Mrs. O. Wikan,
PTA COOKBOOK, Petersburg

Foil-Baked Fish

Place cleaned fish in center of a sheet of foil, add seasonings to taste and a little water. Lay a slice of bacon over the fish, fold the foil to form a tight package, place in hot coals and bake. Time depends upon size of fish.

Helen Benthien, Anchorage

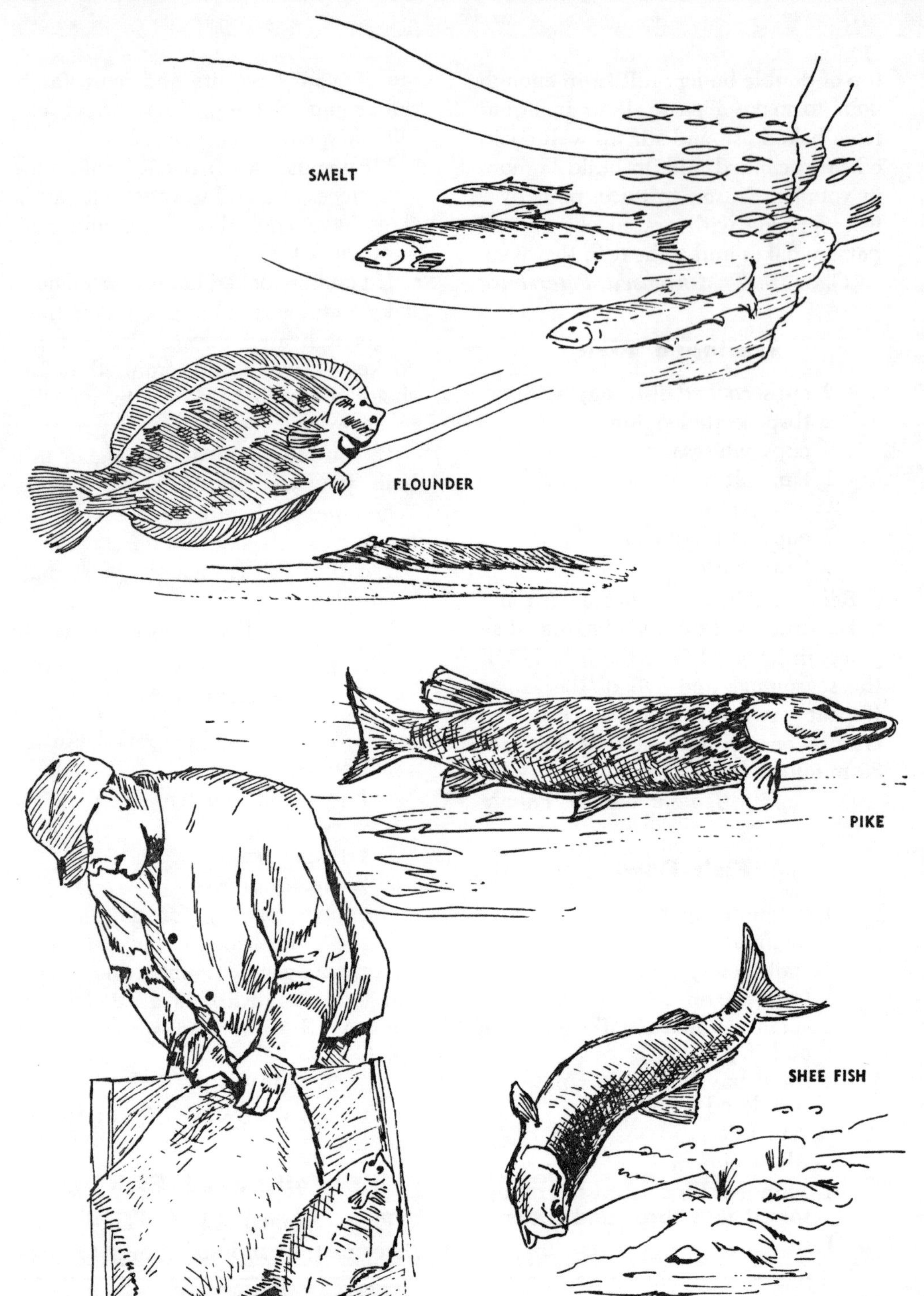
SMELT
FLOUNDER
PIKE
SHEE FISH
HALIBUT

Roast Fish, Injun Style

Clean fish, leaving on head. Shove a sharpened green stick through the gills. Push stick into the ground close to the fire and turn fish frequently so it can cook on both sides. When the skin begins to break or look burned, the fish is done. Remove skin, salt, and serve.

Grouse, ptarmigan and other small birds may be roasted in this way. Singe the bird to remove most of the feathers, remove entrails and wipe body cavity clean. Push the sharpened stick into the base of the bill, and hang beside the fire to roast. When cooked to taste, discard skin, salt and pepper, and serve.

Charles Ricci, Spenard

Fish and Potatoes

Split 1 large fish and lay it, cut side up, on a large piece of heavy foil. (If preferred, cut the fish into serving-size pieces.) Rub surface with 2 tbsp. fat or cooking oil and 1 clove crushed garlic or a minced onion. Turn up the edges of the foil to hold in the juice, and place it on the grill over the coals. Turn fish once. When done, serve with melted butter and lemon, with potatoes on the side.

Potatoes

On one side of a large piece of heavy foil, slice several medium-sized potatoes as for French fries. Add thin slices of raw onion and a clove of garlic, chopped fine. Turn up the edges of the foil so liquid won't run off, then pour ¼ cup cooking oil and 2 tbsp. milk over potatoes. Sprinkle liberally with salt and pepper. Fold the foil over the potatoes and crimp the edges to seal. Place the package on the grill beside the fish. Both should be done in about sixty minutes.

Gussie and Bill Byington, Juneau

Toad in a Hole*

2 eggs
1 cup flour
½ tsp. salt
2 cups milk
1 or 2 drops tabasco sauce
1 or 2 cups cooked fish, leftover or canned

Flake fish and spread in shallow, well-greased baking dish. Make batter of other ingredients, pour over the fish, and bake 30 minutes at 450°. Serve immediately. Serves 4 to 6.

*This dish is reminiscent of a Yorkshire pudding. The original, made with 1½ pounds cubed beefsteak, no tabasco sauce, allegedly came from England where it was a popular beef-stretcher during the postwar austerity period. This adaptation was inspired by the last of a white king salmon baked whole for a large dinner party, but the result was considered worth repeating. Better halve the recipe than make too much for one meal, as it's not so good reheated.

Anonymous, Ketchikan

Best-Ever Fried Salmon

Just fry salmon steaks with a little oil or fat in the pan, do not roll them in flour, cornmeal or anything else, use as little heat as possible and don't try to brown them. Cook until barely done, and season as desired. This way they're juicy, and the tastiest fish you ever lapped a lip over.

Buck Moore, Anchorage

Outdoor Barbecue Salmon

1 white king salmon, 12 to 14 pounds
Salt, pepper, garlic salt

Split fish and remove backbone. Season split sides well with the salt, pepper and garlic salt. Place cut side down on barbecue grill. When your fire is good and hot, put on some green alder. When you have a nice bed of coals, place the grill about a foot above the coals. When the cut side is nicely browned, about 20 minutes, turn carefully and let cook 3 to 4 hours. Delicious, as anyone in Petersburg can testify!

Elsie Clausen, Petersburg, as given to Mamie Jensen, Douglas

Salmon in Cream Tomato Sauce

1 can stewed tomatoes
1 can tomato sauce

Put in a flat pan with a cover, bring to a boil, then turn to simmer. On top of the tomato mixture place salmon split in half, or halibut fillets if you prefer. Salt and pepper, cover, and let cook until fish is barely done. Remove the fish, take off skin and bone (if it's salmon). Thicken the sauce and then add some canned milk, and serve over the fish.

Bob and Alice Thorne, Juneau

Salmon Salad Quickie

1 can salmon or 1 lb. fresh boiled salmon
1 chopped apple
3 tbsp. lemon juice
Salt and pepper
Mayonnaise, lettuce

Break salmon into small chunks, mix with chopped apple and lemon juice, bind with mayonnaise, add salt and pepper. Serve on lettuce.

Hazel Wimer, Elfin Cove

Salmon Fry

Fillet, never slice salmon for frying. Roll fillets in flour and salt to taste. Have pan and oil hot but not too hot. Start frying with skin down and fry to a crisp golden brown before turning. Fry the other side, and put cover on pan until fish is done—just a few minutes. Your fish will be moist and luscious. The secret? The lid!

Norman Rustad, M.V. Nordat

Broiled Kippered Salmon With Egg Sauce

1½ lb. kippered salmon
2 tbsp. butter or other fat, melted
Dash of pepper

Arrange fish skin-side up on preheated, well greased broiler pan and place about 4 inches from source of heat. Broil 7 minutes, turn, baste with butter and sprinkle with pepper. Broil 5 minutes longer, or until brown. Serve with egg sauce. Serves 6.

Egg Sauce

2 tbsp. butter or other fat
2 tbsp. flour
1 cup milk
½ tsp. salt
Dash pepper
3 hard-boiled eggs

Melt butter and blend in flour. Add milk and cook until thick and smooth, stirring constantly. Chop eggs, saving 1 yolk, add chopped eggs and seasoning to sauce, heat, pour over fish and garnish with that other egg yolk, grated.

Norma Norvell, Douglas

Salmon Loaf

To 1 can salmon add 1 cup chopped celery boiled in unsalted water for 10 minutes, ½ cup mayonnaise, 1 cup dry bread crumbs, about 1/3 cup chopped green pepper, 1 small onion, chopped, salt and pepper to taste. Bake in moderate oven about 45 minutes.

This mixture also makes good croquettes or patties.

Can be served with cream sauce or sauce made from 1 can cream of mushroom or cream of celery soup, diluted with ½ can water.

Edna Polley, Juneau

Salmon Patties

- 2 cups cooked salmon
- 1 cup cracker crumbs (Ritz or Hi-Ho)
- 1 small onion, diced
- ½ cup green pepper, diced
- 1 egg
- 1 tsp. salt
- ½ tsp. garlic salt
- ½ tsp. sage
- Pepper to taste

Place all ingredients in large bowl and mix thoroughly. Mixture should be slightly moist and should hold together. If not, add another egg. Form patties, dip in flour and fry in medium-hot skillet until golden brown on each side.

Eva Hager, Sitka

Salmon or Halibut Poached in Sauce

- 1 small onion, chopped
- ½ green pepper, chopped, or a little chopped pimento
- Chopped celery
- 1 tbsp. Worcestershire sauce
- Fish herbs if desired
- Salt and pepper

Bring all to a boil in a small amount of water, in a covered frying pan. On top place seasoned salmon or halibut fillets, cover, and poach until barely done. Lift off fish, remove any skin or bone. Add some milk to the sauce, thicken, and serve over the fish.

Bob and Alice Thorne, Juneau

Smoked Fish

Only fresh, fat sea-run fish are ideal for smoking. In order of quality they are: king salmon, steelhead trout, sockeye, chum, coho (silver) salmon.

First step in preparation is to fillet the fish. Fish under 12 pounds can be smoked "in the side," suspended by the neck end from a wire hook. For larger fish, such as king salmon, cut the flesh side crosswise, following the ribs, at 1-inch intervals. Wash well in cold water.

To 4 gallons water add 3½ qts. rock salt and 1 lb. brown sugar. Stir occasionally until well dissolved. Soak fish 30 minutes in this brine. Lay out on slightly tilted board to drain. Hang fish in the smokehouse by means of wire hooks or heavy white string, not less than 4 feet above fire. Always hang fish with tail end down. This is very important. A baffle of tin about 2 feet above the fire is a good arrangement to divert direct heat and ash from fish.

Green alder is best, and a slow, continuous smoke fire for 40 hours or less, depending upon size of fish and degree of heat. For the first 10 to 12 hours keep the smokehouse door partly open to assure "setting up" of fish and prevent falling. Scrape any excess moss from alder before using.

For kippered salmon, use a lighter brine, dry alder with the bark removed, and less cooking time.

G. S. "Bud" Mortensen, Petersburg

Salmon Heads

Lay salmon heads upside down and

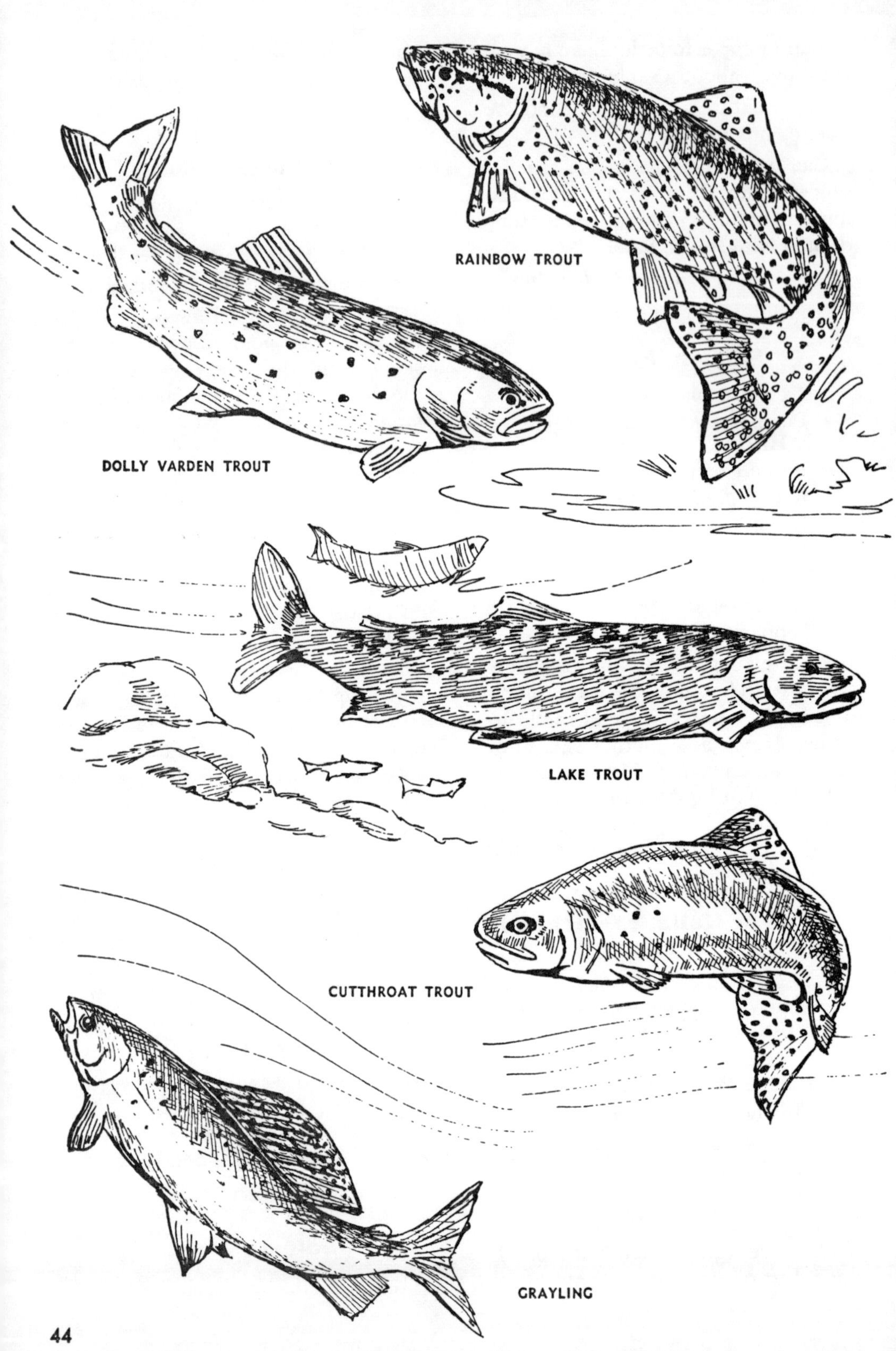
RAINBOW TROUT
DOLLY VARDEN TROUT
LAKE TROUT
CUTTHROAT TROUT
GRAYLING

cut through, taking out gills, eyes and teeth. Fry.

Excellent for making chowder. Put prepared heads in a pot of boiling water, add chopped onions, diced potatoes, tomatoes or tomato sauce or paste, and a little garlic and chopped celery if desired. Bacon, diced and fried, also is a good addition. Cook until vegetables are done.

Lee Hancock, Anchorage

Salmon Backbones

8 5-inch pieces salmon backbone
1 bottle Kraft Casino dressing
1 cup cornmeal

Line cookie sheet with aluminum foil and spread with a thin coating of Casino dressing. Sprinkle backbones with cornmeal, season with salt and a light sprinkle of garlic powder. Place on cookie sheet, each piece lapping just a bit. Spread generously with the rest of the dressing and bake about 45 minutes on the top grate of the oven, turning when first side up is lightly browned.

Vi Haynes, Pelican

Broiled Salmon and Spaghetti

3 large salmon steaks
2 tbsp. melted butter
1 tbsp. sugar
1 cup water
6 oz. long spaghetti
3 tbsp. butter
1 tsp. salt
1/3 cup lemon juice
3 tbsp. flour

Brush salmon steaks with melted butter and place on greased baking pan. Broil about 3 inches from source of heat until fish is easily flaked and moist (5 to 10 minutes on each side). Meanwhile cook spaghetti in boiling salted water until tender, about 15 minutes. Drain and rinse. While the spaghetti cooks, melt the 3 tbsp. butter in a sauce pan, add flour, salt and sugar and stir thoroughly. Add water gradually, stirring constantly, then add lemon juice, still stirring, and cook until thick. Place drained spaghetti on hot platter, cover with sauce and place broiled salmon steaks on top. Garnish and serve. Serves 4 or 5. Easily cooked over campfire.

Louise Juhnke, Chugiak

Salmon Liver

Soak liver overnight in salted water. Next day rinse in clear water, dry, and cut into ¾-inch slices. Season with salt and pepper and fry in butter until golden brown on both sides.

John Hagmeier Sr., Auke Bay

Fishburgers

Remove skin and bone from 1 can salmon, add 2 medium-sized raw potatoes, grated, 2 beaten eggs, 1 medium-sized onion, minced and seasoning to taste, and mix. You'll have a soft batter. Fry it the same as hamburgers, allowing sufficient time for the potato to cook.

Mrs. C. L. Polley, Juneau

Salmon Pie, Russian Style

1 pound can salmon
¼ cup salmon liquor
1 cup cooked rice
1 tbsp. lemon juice
1 medium onion, grated
2 stalks celery, chopped
2 cups pastry mix
2 tbsp. butter or other fat

Drain and flake salmon, reserving liquor. Combine salmon, liquor, rice, lemon juice, onion and celery. Make pastry as directed and line a casserole. Place fish mixture in casserole and dot with butter. Cover casserole with remaining pastry and score top. Bake in a hot oven, 400° F., 45 minutes or until brown. Serves 6.

Salmon Nuggets

1 pound can salmon
½ cup mashed potatoes
1 tbsp. finely minced celery
1 tbsp. grated onion
1 tbsp. butter or other fat, melted
¼ tsp. salt
Dash of pepper
1½ tsp. Worcestershire sauce
1 egg, beaten
¼ pound sharp cheese
1 cup dry bread crumbs

Drain and flake salmon. Combine first 9 ingredients and mix thoroughly. Shape into balls the size of walnuts. Cut cheese into ⅜-inch cubes and insert a cube into the center of each fish ball. Reshape balls and roll in bread crumbs. Fry in deep fat at 375° F. 3 to 4 minutes or until golden brown. Garnish and serve hot, plain or with a sauce. Serves 6.

These may be frozen and heated in the oven just before serving. Freezer temperature should be zero, or lower, and storage time not more than 5 or 6 weeks.

Salmon Kedgeree

2 7-ounce cans smoked salmon
2 cups cooked rice
4 hard-cooked eggs, chopped
¼ cup butter or other fat, melted
¼ cup chopped parsley or dried parsley flakes
½ cup hot milk
Dash of pepper
¼ tsp. salt

Drain and flake salmon, combine all ingredients and heat. Garnish and serve hot. Serves 6.

Barbecued Halibut Sticks

2 pounds halibut steaks or fillets
½ cup salad oil
1 tsp. salt
1 clove garlic, chopped fine
1 cup commercially grated American cheese
1 cup dry bread crumbs

Cut fish into sticks 1 inch by ½ inch by 2 inches. Combine oil, salt and garlic. Place fish in oil mixture for 1 minute. Remove, drain and roll in cheese, then crumbs, and place on a well greased baking pan. Bake in hot oven, 450° F., 12 minutes, or until brown. Garnish and serve hot, plain or with a sauce. Serves 6.

May be frozen and heated in the oven just before serving. Freezer temperature should be zero, or lower, and storage time should be not more than 5 or 6 weeks.

U.S. FWS Bureau of Commercial Fisheries
Technological Laboratory, Ketchikan

Halibut de Luxe

Cut about 2 lbs. halibut into fillets for serving and place in buttered pan. Sprinkle each piece with salt, pepper and garlic salt. Dilute about ½ can cream of mushroom soup with same amount of sherry and pour over fish. Spread with grated cheese. Broil, or bake at 500° for 10 minutes. Sauce may be thickened before serving.

Mrs. H. L. Faulkner, Juneau

Fried Halibut in Wheaties

Using fillet of halibut, dip each piece first in milk, then in crushed

Wheaties. Fry in hot fat, seasoning to taste. Serve with tartar sauce or lemon. The Wheaties give the halibut a different and remarkably good flavor.

Norma Norvell, Douglas

Halibutburgers

- 1 pint cooked halibut, skinned and boned
- 1 slightly beaten egg
- ½ cup cracker crumbs (more if necessary)
- Seasoning to taste

Drain off most of fish liquid, if canned halibut is used. Add slightly beaten egg, seasoning and cracker crumbs and mix well. Form into burgers and fry in moderately hot skillet until brown on each side. This doesn't take long, as the fish is precooked.

Dora Sweeney, Juneau

Halibut Pot Roast

- 3 pound chunk of halibut
- 1 cup flour
- ½ cup cooking oil
- 6 carrots
- 6 medium onions
- ¼ cup butter or other fat
- ¼ cup flour
- 2 cups chopped celery
- 6 potatoes
- 2 cloves garlic, chopped fine
- 2 tsp. salt
- ½ tsp. pepper
- 2 cups water

Remove skin and bones from fish. Roll fish in flour and brown in oil on both sides in a large frying pan or Dutch oven. Place vegetables (previously prepared) around fish and season with salt and pepper. Add water and bake in a moderate oven, 350° F., 1 hour or until fish flakes easily when tested with a fork. Transfer fish and vegetables to a hot platter. Make paste of flour and butter and add it to the liquid, stirring constantly. Pour this gravy over fish and vegetables and serve hot. Serves 6.

This can be cooked easily on a campfire by covering Dutch oven with hot coals.

U.S. FWS Bureau of Commercial Fisheries
Technological Laboratory, Ketchikan

Fried Flounder Fillets

- 2 pounds flounder fillets
- ½ cup flour
- ½ tsp. salt
- 1 tsp. poultry seasoning
- ½ cup milk

Cut fillets into serving portions. Combine flour and seasonings. Dip fish in milk and roll in flour. Fry in fat at a moderate heat until brown on one side. Turn carefully and brown other side. Cooking time about 10 minutes depending upon thickness of fish. Drain on absorbent paper, garnish and serve hot, plain or with a sauce. Serves 6.

Flounder Dinner in Aluminum Foil

- 2 pounds flounder fillets
- 1 pound tomatoes, peeled and sliced
- 1½ cups sliced potatoes
- 3 tsp. salt
- 6 slices bacon, chopped
- 2 tbsp. chopped onion
- 1½ cups sliced green beans
- Dash pepper

Cut fish into serving-size portions. Measure and cut 6 18-inch pieces of foil. In center of each arrange 1/6 of fish, bacon, tomato, potato, onion and green beans. Sprinkle with salt and pepper. Wrap securely and seal well, place on a bed of hot coals and cook 20 minutes, turning frequently for even cooking. Serve hot in foil. Serves 6.

Rockfish

Of about 20 different species of rockfish found in the North Pacific (some erroneously called red snapper), the skin color varies from dark gray to bright orange but the flesh varies little in flavor. It is lean, meaty, firm, and when cooked it is white and forms large flakes. Rockfish is enough like crab in texture and flavor that it is often used as a substitute for crab. It is also widely used for "fish and chips." Excellent when oven-fried by the Spencer Hot Oven method at the beginning of fish section.

Baked Stuffed Rockfish Rolls

2 pounds (or 6) rockfish fillets
1 tsp. salt
Dash pepper
1 tbsp. lemon juice
½ cup flour
Favorite recipe, bread stuffing

Sprinkle fillets with salt, pepper and lemon juice. Place a ball of stuffing on each fillet, roll and tie securely with string. Roll in flour and brown in hot fat. Place rolls in a well greased, covered casserole and bake in moderate oven, 350° F., 30 minutes or until fish flakes easily when tested with a fork. Remove string, garnish and serve hot. Serves 6.

Rockfish Fillets in Sour Sauce

2 pounds rockfish fillets
1 tsp. salt
2 tbsp. lemon juice
¼ cup milk
½ cup flour

Cut fillets into serving-size portions, sprinkle with salt and lemon juice, and allow to stand 10 minutes in milk. Roll fillets in flour and fry in deep fat, 375° F., until brown. Drain on absorbent paper and serve with sour sauce. Serves 6.

Sour Sauce

2 tbsp. butter or other fat
2 tbsp. flour
½ tsp. salt
Dash pepper
1 cup milk
2 eggs, beaten
1 tbsp. lemon juice
½ cup mushrooms

Melt fat, blend in flour and seasonings, add milk gradually and cook, stirring constantly, until thick and smooth. Stir a little of the hot sauce into beaten egg, then add remaining sauce, stirring constantly. Just before serving, stir in lemon juice and mushrooms. Serves 6.

Broiled Sablefish (Black Cod)

2 pounds sablefish fillets
1 tsp. salt
1 tsp. lemon juice
2 tbsp. butter or other fat, melted

Cut fish into serving-size portions and sprinkle with salt and lemon juice. Place on a preheated, well greased broiler rack, brush with fat, broil about 2 inches from source of heat for 12 minutes, or until fish flakes easily when tested with a fork. Garnish and serve hot. Serves 6.

Boiled Sablefish Fillets

2 pounds sablefish fillets
½ tsp. salt
2 tbsp. butter or other fat, melted
1 8-ounce can tomato sauce

1 large onion, finely chopped
½ cup grated cheddar cheese

Cut fish into serving-size portions, sprinkle with salt, place in a well greased baking pan and brush with melted fat. Broil in a preheated broiler 8 minutes. Pour tomato sauce over fish, sprinkle with onion and cheese and broil 4 minutes longer, or until cheese melts. Garnish and serve hot. Serves 6.

Fried Smelt or Eulachon ("Hooligan")

18 smelt
1 tbsp. salt
1 cup milk
¾ cup flour
¾ cup dry bread crumbs

Remove heads and viscera of smelt. Wash and drain. Add salt to milk. Sift flour and crumbs together. Dip fish in milk and roll in flour mixture, then fry in fat at a moderate heat until brown on one side. Turn carefully and brown other side. Cooking time about 10 minutes, depending upon thickness of fish. Drain on absorbent paper, garnish and serve hot, plain or with a sauce. Serves 6.

Poached Smelt with Brown Gravy

18 smelt
1½ tsp. salt
2 slices lemon
1 pint boiling water
2 tbsp. butter or other fat
2 tbsp. flour

Fillet smelt, roll each fillet and fasten with toothpicks. Place rolls in sauce pan, add 1 tsp. salt and the lemon slices to the boiling water, and pour over fish. Simmer 10 minutes or until fish flakes easily when tested with a fork. Remove fish to a hot platter. Melt fat in sauce pan, blend in flour and remaining salt, and stir constantly until brown. Add liquid from fish, stirring until thick and smooth. Pour gravy over fish and serve hot. Serves 6.

U.S. FWS Bureau of Commercial Fisheries
Technological Laboratory, Ketchikan

"Hooligan" Casserole

Clean and wash eulachon and place a layer in a greased casserole. Chop fine 1 onion and 1 clove garlic, sprinkle some and some salt and pepper over the fish and cover with a ¼-inch layer of cracker crumbs. Continue layers until casserole is full. Pour 1 cup whole milk over all and bake in moderately hot oven (350° to 400° F.) for 1 to 1½ hours or until fish flake easily when tested with a fork.

Frank "Buck" Moore, Anchorage

Stuffed Whitefish

Select a fresh 6-pound whitefish, clean it, and stuff it as you would a turkey with your favorite bread dressing. Fry some bacon until the grease runs freely. Slash the outside of the fish through the skin in several places, insert 6 half-cloves of garlic, pour the bacon and bacon fat over the fish, and bake in a hot oven until done.

Rev. Joseph McElmeel, S.J., Sitka
(The late "Father Mac" was for more than thirty years a missionary priest in the Nulato area.)

Pickled Herring

Wash the herring, scale thoroughly and rewash. Remove entrails and cut off heads and tails. Salt herring down in a wooden keg, alternating a layer of rock salt and a layer of herring. Let them sit for not less than 1 week, not more than 2 weeks. Remove herring from keg, wash thoroughly, and salt again in the keg. After another week wash the herring thoroughly and soak overnight in cold water, changing the water several times to remove all the salt. Cut herring into chunks about 1 inch long.

Into a clean pint jar place 1 tsp. dark brown sugar, then alternate layers of herring chunks with layers of thinly sliced onion and lemon and a sprinkling of pickling spices (allow 1 level tsp. spices to 1 pint). Press down firmly and fill jar to ½ inch from the top with vinegar (full strength or diluted with water according to your taste). Allow time for the vinegar to seep in, then pour in more to bring it to the former level. Seal the jars firmly, store in a cool place, and turn each day to insure thorough mixing of spices. This is ready to eat in 2 weeks, but keeps almost indefinitely under refrigeration.

Eva Hagar, Sitka

Picnic Trout

Clean the freshly caught trout, season with salt and pepper, wrap in foil and bake on a bed of coals for 15 minutes or longer depending upon the size of the trout. Serve with dill pickles, potato chips and sliced tomatoes. (Better have the makings for hot dogs along, just in case the fish aren't biting!)

Kathryn Hagmeier, Auke Bay

Baked Trout

1 large trout
1 onion, sliced thick
1 stalk celery, chopped
Sliced American cheese
Top milk or cream
Flour
Salt and pepper
1 tbsp. Worcestershire or steak sauce

Clean the trout, dry it thoroughly inside and out, slit it nearly all the way down one side, season with salt and pepper and dredge with flour. Lay it in a buttered oblong pan, slit side up. Place a layer of sliced onions inside fish, flour slightly, place slices of cheese on top of onions, and celery on top of cheese. Flour slightly to thicken. Season with salt, pepper and sauce and close body cavity with toothpicks. Place remaining slices of onion on top of trout, moisten the top with the milk or cream and pour the rest into the pan beside trout. Bake uncovered in slow oven, allowing liquid to thicken. Baste occasionally and cook until done.

Mrs. James Nolan, Wrangell

Fried Trout with Spanish Sauce

1 trout, 2½ to 3 pounds
6 cloves garlic, chopped fine (optional)
½ cup chopped onion
1 tomato, chopped, or ½ can tomato sauce
2 tbsp. butter or other fat, melted

Fry onion and garlic in fat until tender. Add tomato and cook 5 minutes longer. Roll fish in flour and brown on both sides; pour sauce over fish, cover, and cook slowly for 10 minutes or until fish flakes easily when tested with a fork. Serves 6.

U.S. FWS Bureau of Commercial Fisheries
Technological Laboratory, Ketchikan

Chapter **9**

SHELLFISH

Dungeness and King Crab Butchering

Use only live, healthy crabs. Crabs are preferably butchered and cleaned before precooking. Use a sturdy, flat-topped table with a sharp, square edge. Hold the underside of the crab on the table edge, keeping the mid-line parallel with the edge. Grasp the legs and, with a slight twisting motion, pull quickly down and away from the back or carapace.

Tear off back. With large crabs a stationary butchering iron or hook may be used to tear off back before breaking in half.

Trim off gills and viscera, being careful not to contaminate meat with viscera, which results in off flavor and discoloration in the finished product. Wash each section thoroughly under running, cold water. Do not soak.

Precooking

Precook in boiling salted water (½ cup salt per gallon of water) for 10 minutes, or steam in pressure cooker at 212° F. (no pressure) for 13 to 15 minutes. Large crabs (king or whole dungeness) should be cooked 5 minutes longer. Do not overcook, as it tends to cause excessive shrinkage of meat.

If a quantity of crabs is being boiled, change the water frequently to prevent concentration of blood and other coagulated proteins.

Remove from boiling water or steamer and cool quickly by dipping briefly in clean, cold water or spraying for about 2 minutes with cold water. This helps to firm and shrink the meat, making it easier to remove from the shell.

Picking

Pick the meat as soon as possible after cooking, before it is cold. Shake meat into aluminum, stainless steel, galvanized or enamelware pans, never copper or iron.

To remove body meat, grasp the legs firmly and knock rather hard against the side of the pan, breaking or crushing the bony structure. This is messy, but the best and fastest way.

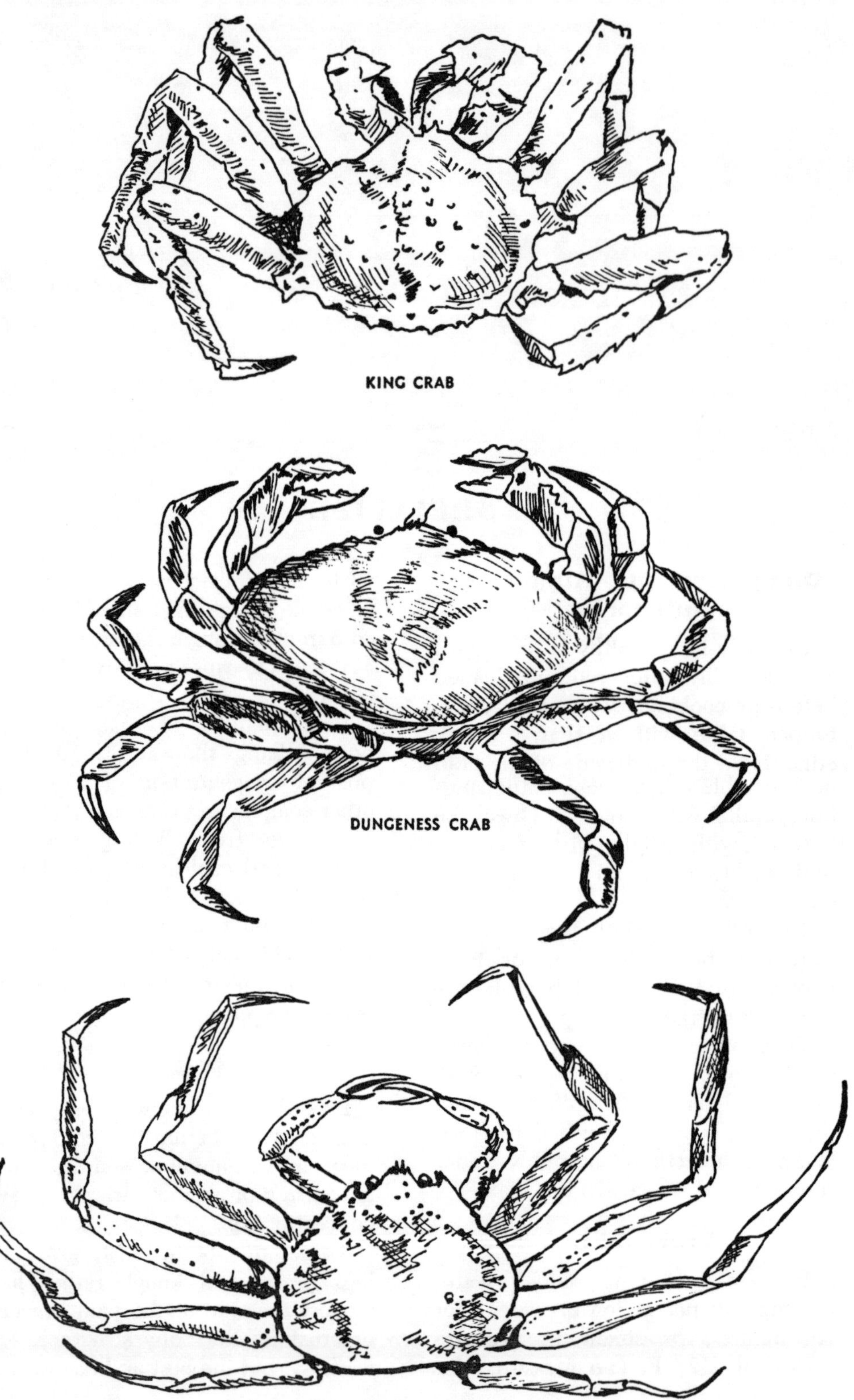

KING CRAB

DUNGENESS CRAB

TANNER CRAB

To remove leg meat, start with the small tip at end of each leg and work toward the large end. Pull off the tip and cartilaginous tendon which connects it to the adjacent section, and discard. Break shell in each section with a wooden hammer, and knock pieces of meat into the pan, trying to keep the pieces whole.

To remove claw meat, pull out the small jointed pincher of the claw along with the cartilaginous tendon which connects it with the large claw section. Crack claw with wooden hammer and shake meat out in whole pieces.

Crab, Alaska Fisherman's Style

1 pound crab meat
½ cup chopped onion
1 clove garlic, chopped fine
1½ tbsp. chopped parsley
¼ cup chopped celery
¼ cup butter or other fat, melted
¾ cup canned tomatoes
1 cup tomato sauce
¾ cup water
¼ tsp. pepper
¼ tsp. paprika
½ tsp. chili powder
4½ cups cooked spaghetti
½ cup grated cheese

Remove any shell or cartilage, being careful not to break meat more than necessary. Cook onion, garlic, parsley and celery in fat until tender. Add tomatoes, water and seasonings and simmer 1 hour. Add crab meat and simmer 10 minutes longer. Stir in spaghetti. Serve hot with cheese sprinkled over the top. Serves 6.

Crab Salad

2 cups crab meat
½ cup mayonnaise or salad dressing
1 cup chopped celery
2 tsp. chopped sweet pickle
1 tbsp. chopped onion
2 hard-boiled eggs, chopped
Dash pepper
½ tsp. salt
Lettuce
Tomato

Remove any shell or cartilage, being careful not to break meat more than necessary. Combine all ingredients. Serve on lettuce, garnished with tomato wedges and leg meat. Serves 6.

Green Peppers Stuffed with Crab

1 cup crab meat
4 green peppers
2 slices bacon, chopped
½ cup chopped onion
¾ cup chopped celery
1 cup soft breadcrumbs
2 eggs, beaten
½ tsp. salt
Dash pepper
¼ cup grated cheese

Remove any shell or cartilage and flake crab meat. Cut a thin slice from the stem end of each pepper and remove seeds. Simmer peppers in boiling, salted water 5 to 8 minutes, or until almost tender. Drain. Fry bacon until crisp. Add onion and celery and cook until these are tender. Add breadcrumbs and cook 3 minutes longer. Add eggs, seasonings and crab meat. Fill peppers with crab mixture, sprinkle cheese over tops and bake in hot oven, 400° F., 20 minutes or until cheese melts. Serves 4.

U.S. FWS Bureau of Commercial Fisheries
Technological Laboratory, Ketchikan

Hot Crab Souffle

8 slices bread

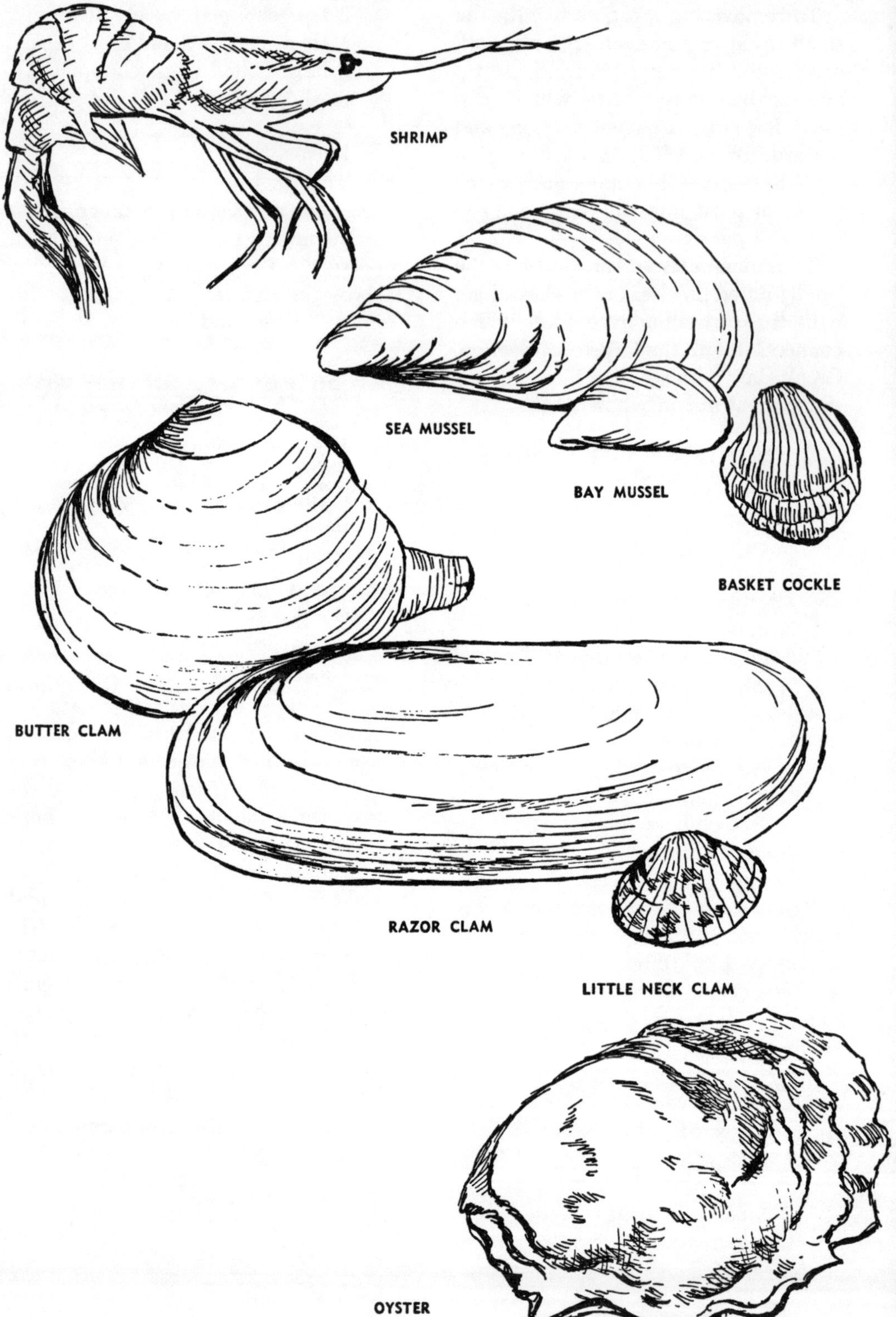

SHRIMP

SEA MUSSEL

BAY MUSSEL

BASKET COCKLE

BUTTER CLAM

RAZOR CLAM

LITTLE NECK CLAM

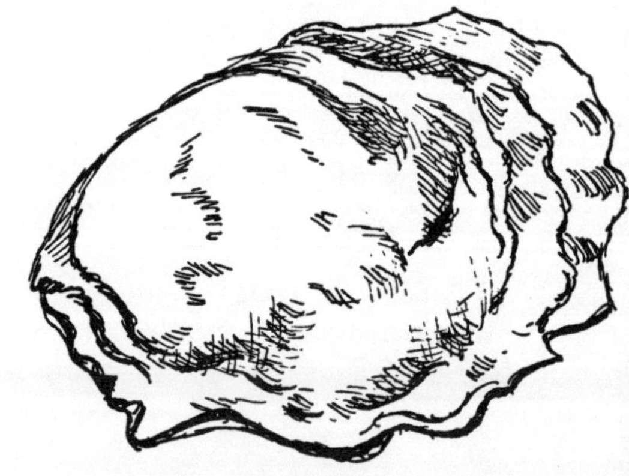

OYSTER

2 cups crab or shrimp
½ cup mayonnaise
1 onion, chopped
1 green pepper, chopped
1 cup celery, chopped
3 cups milk
4 eggs
1 can cream of mushroom soup
Grated cheese
Paprika

Dice half of bread into greased baking dish. Mix crab (or shrimp), mayonnaise, onion, green pepper and celery and spread over diced bread. Trim crusts from remaining 4 slices of bread and place trimmed slices over seafood mixture. Mix eggs and milk and pour over the top, and place in refrigerator overnight. Bake 15 minutes at 325° F. Pour soup over top, sprinkle on cheese and paprika, and bake 1 hour.

Mrs. Kenneth Junge, Juneau

Crab for Breakfast

Melt butter in a skillet, brown bits of crab in it, then add beaten eggs and proceed as for scrambled eggs. Very different, and very good.

Jacques Norvell, Douglas

Crab Soup

1 cup crab meat
½ cup sherry
1 can tomato soup
1 can pea soup
1 soup can of light cream
¼ tsp. curry powder
¼ tsp. sugar
½ tsp. paprika

Put crab in a bowl, pour wine over it and let stand 1 hour. Blend tomato and pea soups, heat to boiling point, add seasonings and ½ tsp. soda, remove from heat, and when it stops bubbling add cream and crab. Reheat slowly but do not allow to boil.

Mrs. Bertha Meier, Anchorage

Fried Crab Legs, Shrimp or Prawns

2 tbsp. flour
2 tbsp. cornmeal
Salt and pepper
1 egg
1 tbsp. or more water
Pinch of baking powder

Beat together with rotary beater for a minute or so, or shake well in a jar with a tight lid. Dump in seafood, to have it well covered with batter. Fry at medium heat in about 1 inch of shortening until golden brown, turn, and fry on other side only until done.

Mamie Jensen, Douglas

Campers' Delight

1 can crab
1 can shrimp
1 can mushrooms
1 chopped green pepper
2 cups chopped celery, or 1 can mixed Chinese vegetables
¼ cup chopped pimento

Cook green pepper and celery in small amount of water until almost tender. Combine with other ingredients and pour into white sauce made as follows: Melt 2 tbsp. margarine over low fire, add 2 tbsp. flour, ½ tsp. salt, a dash of pepper and a dash of paprika, then slowly stir in 1 cup milk and cook until thick. (A can of cream of celery or cream of mushroom soup diluted with ½ can of water may be substituted for the white sauce.) Reheat entire mixture and serve on toast or rice.

Mrs. Steve Beers, Ketchikan

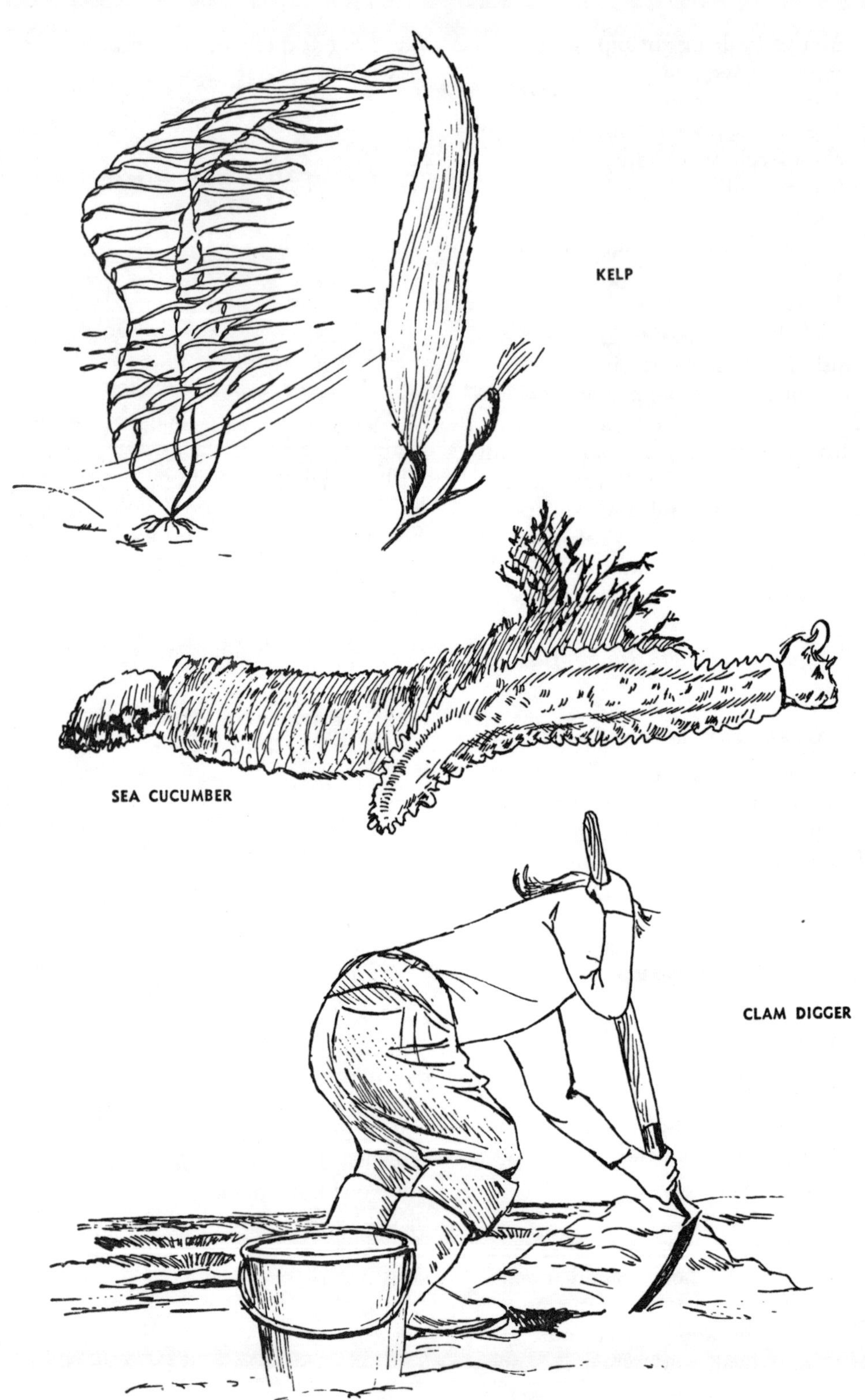
KELP
SEA CUCUMBER
CLAM DIGGER

Shrimp Salad

1 pound shrimp meat, diced
1 stalk celery
2 green peppers
1 can pimento
½ cup broken walnut meats
½ head lettuce, shredded
Mayonnaise or French dressing

Dice celery, peppers and pimento, add walnuts and shrimp, mix well with dressing and let stand 2 hours before serving. Serve on lettuce.

Charles Greenaa, from
PTA COOKBOOK, Petersburg

Easy Shrimp Creole

¼ cup finely chopped celery
1 medium onion, chopped
3 tbsp. salad oil
¾ cup Campbell's tomato soup
½ cup water
¼ tsp. garlic salt
1 tsp. vinegar
1 cup fresh, cooked shrimp or 7-ounce can shrimp
2 cups cooked rice

Cook celery and onion in salad oil until soft. Blend in the water, soup, salt and vinegar and simmer about 10 minutes. Add shrimp, reheat, and serve over hot rice. Or add the rice to the creole and heat together before serving. Serves 4.

Mamie Jensen, Douglas

French Fried Shrimp

1½ pounds raw shrimp
2 eggs, beaten
¾ tsp. salt
2 cups dry breadcrumbs
Fat for deep frying

Peel shrimp and remove sand veins. Wash and cut almost through lengthwise. Combine egg and salt. Roll shrimp in crumbs, dip in egg mixture and roll again in crumbs. Fry in deep fat at 375° F. for 2 to 3 minutes, or until golden brown. Drain on absorbent paper, garnish, and serve plain or with sauce. Serves 6.

French Fried Shrimp Pasteles

1 pound raw shrimp
1½ cups flour
1 cup milk
1 tsp. salt
½ cup grated onion
5 cloves garlic, chopped fine (optional)

Peel shrimp and remove sand veins. Wash and cut in half lengthwise. Combine flour, milk and salt. Add onions, garlic and shrimp. Drop by teaspoonfuls into deep fat, 375° F., and fry 2 to 3 minutes, or until golden brown. Drain on absorbent paper. Garnish and serve hot. Serves 6.

Curried Shrimp

1 pound shrimp, cooked, peeled and cleaned
¼ cup butter or other fat
¼ cup flour
1½ tsp. curry powder
Dash cayenne
2 cups milk
2 egg yolks, beaten
3 cups cooked rice
Salt

Melt fat, blend in flour and seasonings, add milk gradually, stirring constantly, and cook until thick and smooth. Stir a little of the hot sauce into the egg yolks, then add yolks to remaining sauce, stirring constantly. Add shrimp, salt to taste, reheat and serve in rice ring. Serves 6.

U.S. FWS Bureau of Commercial Fisheries
Technological Laboratory, Ketchikan

Marinated Shrimp

Combine ¾ cup salad oil, ¾ of a small jar hot mustard, ½ cup vinegar, 2 or 3 teaspoons paprika, 3 chopped green onions, and salt and pepper to taste. Pour over Alaskan salad shrimp, covering well. Allow to marinate 12 hours or more in the refrigerator or cool place. Serve cold. Freshly cooked Dungeness crab meat is also good prepared this way.

G. S. "Bud" Mortensen, Petersburg

Broiled Garlic Shrimp

2 pounds fresh or frozen shrimp, jumbo size
¼ pound butter or margarine
1 clove garlic, minced

Remove shells from uncooked shrimp and cut out sand veins. Butterfly shrimp and arrange in baking dish or on foil with sides folded up. Melt butter, add garlic, simmer for three minutes, pour over the shrimp and broil for 5 minutes. Sprinkle with salt and serve.

Virginia Koppinger, Anchorage

Pickled Shrimp

1 pound shelled raw shrimp
Vinegar to cover (about 2 cups)
1 tbsp. dry mustard
1 tbsp. cayenne pepper
¼ box celery seed
3 or 4 bay leaves

Put all seasoning in the vinegar and bring to a boil. Add raw shrimp. Bring to a boil again and boil for 15 minutes. When shrimp can be speared with a fork they are done. Put shrimp in a clean jar, cover with the liquid, seal, and place in refrigerator. They keep indefinitely, and improve with age.

Teen Cox, Skagway

Barbecued Oysters

1 pint (about 12) select oysters
½ cup salad oil
1 tsp. salt
1 clove garlic, chopped fine
½ cup commercially grated American cheese
½ cup dry breadcrumbs

Drain oysters. Combine oil, salt and garlic. Place oysters in oil mixture and leave 1 minute. Remove, drain and roll in grated cheese. Roll in crumbs and place in a well-greased baking pan. Bake in hot oven, 450° F., 12 minutes or until brown. Garnish and serve hot, plain or with a sauce. Serves 6.

Broiled Oysters on the Half Shell

36 oysters in the shell
½ tsp. salt
Dash pepper
½ cup dry breadcrumbs
2 tbsp. butter or other fat, melted

Shuck and drain oysters. Scrub deep halves of shells thoroughly. Place an oyster on each shell, sprinkle with salt and pepper. Combine fat and crumbs and sprinkle over oysters. Place on preheated broiler pan about 3 inches from the source of heat and broil 5 minutes, or until brown. Serves 6.

Curried Oysters

1 pint oysters
½ cup chopped onion
2 tbsp. butter or other fat
3 tbsp. flour
1½ cups milk
2 hard-cooked eggs, sliced
¾ tsp. salt
Dash pepper
1 tsp. curry powder
3 cups cooked rice

Simmer oysters in their liquor for 5 minutes or until edges curl. Drain.

Cook onion in fat until tender, blend in flour, add milk gradually and cook until thick, stirring constantly. Add eggs, seasonings and oysters, heat, and serve hot in a rice ring. Serves 6.

Oyster Stew

1 pint oysters
¼ cup butter or other fat
1 quart oyster liquor and milk
1½ tsp. salt
Dash pepper

Drain oysters, reserving liquor. Melt fat, add oysters and cook 3 minutes, or until edges curl. Add liquid, salt and pepper and heat almost to boiling. Garnish and serve hot. Serves 6.

U.S. FWS Bureau of Commercial Fisheries
Technological Laboratory, Ketchikan

Scalloped Oysters or Salmon

2 slices bread, crumbled fine
1 egg, well beaten
1½ cup milk (or 1 cup canned milk and ½ cup water)
Seasoning to taste
12 large oysters cut in half, or 1 large can salmon

Put ingredients in well-buttered casserole and bake slowly, 300° F., until firm like custard.

Mrs. Sylvia Collins

How to Prepare Clams

The first step is the cleaning process, and there is no satisfactory shortcut. Put the clams in a burlap bag, tie it near the top with a strong rope, and suspend it from the boat or float in salt water for 20 to 30 hours.

Next comes the shucking. An ordinary old case knife is best. Never use a sharp knife. It is unnecessary and hazardous. Work the blade inside the shell, keeping it pressed to shell, and sever the muscle. Repeat on the opposite side. Discard the neck and loose, jelly-like substance along with the shell.

Wash in clear water and place in a colander to drain. Clams are now ready for general use, and should be considered as perishable as fresh trout.

Clam Fritters

4 eggs
2 cups clams and liquor
1 cup flour
2 tsp. baking powder
Salt

Beat eggs until frothy; grind enough fresh clams to make 2 cups clams and juice, and add to eggs. Add flour, baking powder and salt, sifted together, and fry like pan cakes on a hot, well-buttered griddle. If batter is too thick, thin with water. Serve as a main dish.

Clam Chowder

1 cup chopped bacon or ham
½ cup chopped salt pork
2 cups chopped onions
2 cups chopped celery
1 cup chopped carrots
2 tbsp. butter
2 tbsp. flour
1 quart boiling water or ham broth
3 cups diced raw potatoes
Salt and pepper
½ lemon
2 quarts coarse-cut raw clams

Braise ham or bacon and salt pork in a heavy pot until half fried. Add onions, celery and carrot, stir occasionally, and braise until vegetables are half cooked. Pour off excess fat, then add the butter, let it melt, then add flour and when well blended, add boiling water or broth. Allow to simmer 1 hour. Add the diced raw potatoes and seasonings. When potatoes are tender, add the lemon and clams. Never, but never let clams cook more than 12 minutes! Yield, 1 gallon.

When serving this chowder, put a can of allspice on the table for the individual whim.

For variation, add tomatoes or milk. If tomatoes, omit some of the water; if milk, use straight canned milk and add at the very last.

G.S. "Bud" Mortensen, Petersburg

Broiled Clams on the Half Shell

Use small butter clams. Give them a quick scrubbing with a brush. Starting knife edge at the front, split straight back to hinge. If necks were already well out, cut them off before you scrub and split the clams. Otherwise, snip off the black part of the split neck with a pair of scissors. Wash out the sand under the cold water tap, leaving no water. Then break the hinge, leaving 2 half-clams in half-shells.

Do this with about three times as many clams as you think those present will eat. Then arrange them on big, shallow baking tins, put a dot of butter and a sprinkle of garlic salt on each half-clam. Place under broiler or in a very hot oven for 3 to 5 minutes, until they just start to curl brown at the edges. The smaller ones may get quite browned, which is good for variety. Eat at once, and drink the bit of nectar in the shell. Most flavorsome and only really tender cooked clams.

Dick Brennan,
PTA COOKBOOK, Petersburg

Clam Patties

1 quart ground clams
10 eggs (unbeaten)
About 50 crackers, crumbled
Salt and pepper to taste

Mix all ingredients in a bowl or pan, with a fork. Do not beat. Fry one for testing. It should be firm and should turn easily. If it breaks, add. more cracker crumbs or another egg. (This is an original recipe, and I have never written down the exact amounts. They can vary with the size of the eggs and the amount of liquor on the clams.) Diced onion or green pepper may be added, but in this recipe we prefer the full clam flavor. Fry in hot margarine or butter but do not overcook. Turn only once.

Mrs. Olaf Winther, Pelican

Clam and Rice Casserole

¼ cup butter
1 cup minced onion
2 4-ounce cans mushrooms, sliced and drained
Seasoned salt
Pepper
1 cup dry white wine
1 cup raw white rice
1 pint clams
½ cup Parmesan cheese

Melt butter, add onions and mushrooms, sprinkle with 1½ tsp. seasoned salt and ⅛ tsp. pepper, and sauté 15 minutes. Add wine and simmer slowly, uncovered, for 15 minutes. Cook rice (not minute rice) as usual and drain well. Combine rice and onion-mushroom mixture. In greased casserole place a layer of the mixture and then a layer of drained clams. Sprinkle the top with seasoned salt, pepper and grated cheese. Bake for 30 minutes. If desired, place under the broiler before serving to brown the top more.

Sam H. Roberson, Douglas

John's Clam Chowder

3 or 4 pieces bacon, diced

2 or 3 onions, chopped fine
Potatoes, diced (one per person)
Clams, diced, as many as you want
Milk

Fry bacon until crisp, add onions, potatoes, clams, salt, and water to cover. Cook until potatoes are done. Heat the milk separately. Ladle the clam mixture into bowls and pour the hot milk over it. This way the clam mixture doesn't sour if there's any left over.

Kathryn Hagmeier, Juneau

Clam Fritters

2 cups biscuit mix
2/3 cup milk
1 egg
2 cups minced clams

Mix first three ingredients (batter will be lumpy), stir in clams, drop by small teaspoonful into hot fat (360 to 375° F.), turn, and brown on both sides. Drain on absorbent paper. Makes about 2 dozen fritters. Easy, and a favorite.

Mrs. A. N. Decker, Hoonah

Kenny's Chowder

Dice potatoes, celery, carrots and onion in amounts and proportions to suit your taste and the number of mouths you plan to feed, and boil in water to cover until potatoes and carrots are almost done. Add some minced parsley, a bit of pimento and a dash of garlic, then add bite-sized chunks of halibut, black cod or any other raw fish you like. Simmer gently until fish is cooked, then add minced razor clams, canned shrimp, small oysters, and a generous amount of bacon, chopped and fried, with some of its fat. Heat it through, but don't boil it again. Add enough evaporated milk to make it rich and creamy, and salt, pepper and butter to taste. Serve piping hot, with a dash of paprika on top of each serving.

This is just as good warmed up the next day. You can make it with razor clams alone, but it takes lots of clams.

Kenny Thompson, Haines

Clamburgers

1 cup chopped clams
1 egg, beaten
1 tbsp. lemon juice
1 tbsp. chopped parsley
1 tbsp. grated onion
½ tsp. salt
Dash of pepper
½ cup dried breadcrumbs
6 buttered buns

Combine all ingredients except buns. Form into 6 flat cakes, fry in fat at moderate heat until brown on one side, turn carefully and brown other side. Cooking time about 10 minutes. Serve in heated buns. Makes 6.

Clam Dip

1 7-ounce can minced razor clams
1 cup cream, whipped
1 4-ounce package cream cheese
Salt, pepper and grated onion to taste
Potato chips

Drain clams. Combine all ingredients except potato chips. Serve chilled in a bowl surrounded with potato chips. Makes about 1 pint dip.

U.S. FWS Bureau of Commercial Fisheries
Technological Laboratory, Ketchikan

Baked Clams

1 onion
1 green pepper

2 stalks celery
Potato chips
Salt and pepper
2 slices bacon, diced

Use a flat, shallow casserole or pan. Chop the onion, green pepper and celery. Fry bacon until crisp, remove from the pan and brown the vegetables lightly in the bacon fat. Cover the bottom of the casserole with small clams (removed from shell), add the vegetable mixture, top with more clams, salt and pepper, then sprinkle with crushed potato chips and crisp bacon. Bake 20 or 30 minutes.

Gussie and Bill Byington, Juneau

Risotto with Clams

¼ cup cooking oil
1 onion, chopped fine
1 clove garlic, chopped fine
2 cups canned tomatoes (clam broth may furnish part of this quantity)
2 tbsp. chopped parsley (optional)
Pinch of basil (optional)
1 cup raw rice
¾ tsp. salt
2 cups minced clams, or equivalent in fresh clams in shell

Sauté onions and garlic lightly in oil, add all but the clams, cover tightly and steam until rice is tender but not soft, about 15 to 20 minutes. Add clams, cover, and heat until flavors are blended.

When fresh clams are used, place well-scrubbed clams on top of rice, cover, and steam until shells open.

Eunice and Ray Nevin, Juneau

Sea Cucumber Dip

For the ultimate in seafood dips, substitute sea cucumber for razor clams in the above recipe. Catch a sea cucumber with a dip net, spear it with a pike pole, or jig it with a halibut hook. The flavor is well worth the effort. Rip it open, remove the long, thin white muscles that run lengthwise down the middle, and discard all the rest. Cook muscles for a few minutes, until they look done, then mince, grind, or whip in a blender, drain, and use. The muscles of one sea cucumber are enough for one recipe of dip.

If you don't tell your guests what the secret ingredient is until after they've tasted the dip, they'll wish you had caught two sea cucumbers and doubled the recipe.

Anonymous, Ketchikan

Blue Mussels

In many Alaskan bays and inlets the large blue mussel is to be found in great numbers. The smaller mussels are common too, but of little food value. The larger variety is easy to locate at low tide, in heavy clusters growing fast to large rocks and ledges. The ideal size, 2 to 3 inches long, is easy to break loose by hand (gloves recommended). Mussels are better gathered during the "R months," as during May, June, July and August there is more likelihood of "red tide" poisoning. Alaskan waters are so cold, however, that the quality of any shellfish is good at any time of year.

Aristocrat of Sea Food Chowders

First wash the mussels in salt water, then in clear water. Place only one layer in a shallow pan, season with salt and pepper, and barely cover with water. Allow to simmer 20 minutes, or until the shells open up. Cook plenty of mussels, save the cooking water, and discard the shells. Using my basic recipe for clam chowder (second clam recipe in this section), substitute the cooking liquid for the water and mussels for clams, adding the mussels to the chowder last. A pinch of dried parsley flakes improves any chowder.

Mussels in Butter

Wash mussels and cook, as for chowder, until shells open, and serve in the shells with a dip made of melted butter and lemon juice, and small forks or toothpicks for eating implements. The cooking liquid is an excellent hot drink.

G.S. "Bud" Mortensen, Petersburg

"Rock Oyster" Stew, Camp Style

1 package dehydrated onion soup
1 package dehydrated potatoes
6 slices bacon
Salt and pepper
Milk
½ bushel blue mussels, about 2 quarts when steamed and shelled

Steam mussels in a large pot until shells open. Remove meat and toss out shells and liquid.

Fry bacon until crisp, drain on paper towels, then crumble.

Prepare onion soup according to directions on package, thicken with potato powder, and simmer until potatoes are done. Dilute to chowder consistency with milk, which may be canned or reconstituted. Add mussels and heat thoroughly but do not boil. Season to taste with salt and pepper, add crumbled bacon, and serve hot with crackers.

Sam H. Roberson, Douglas

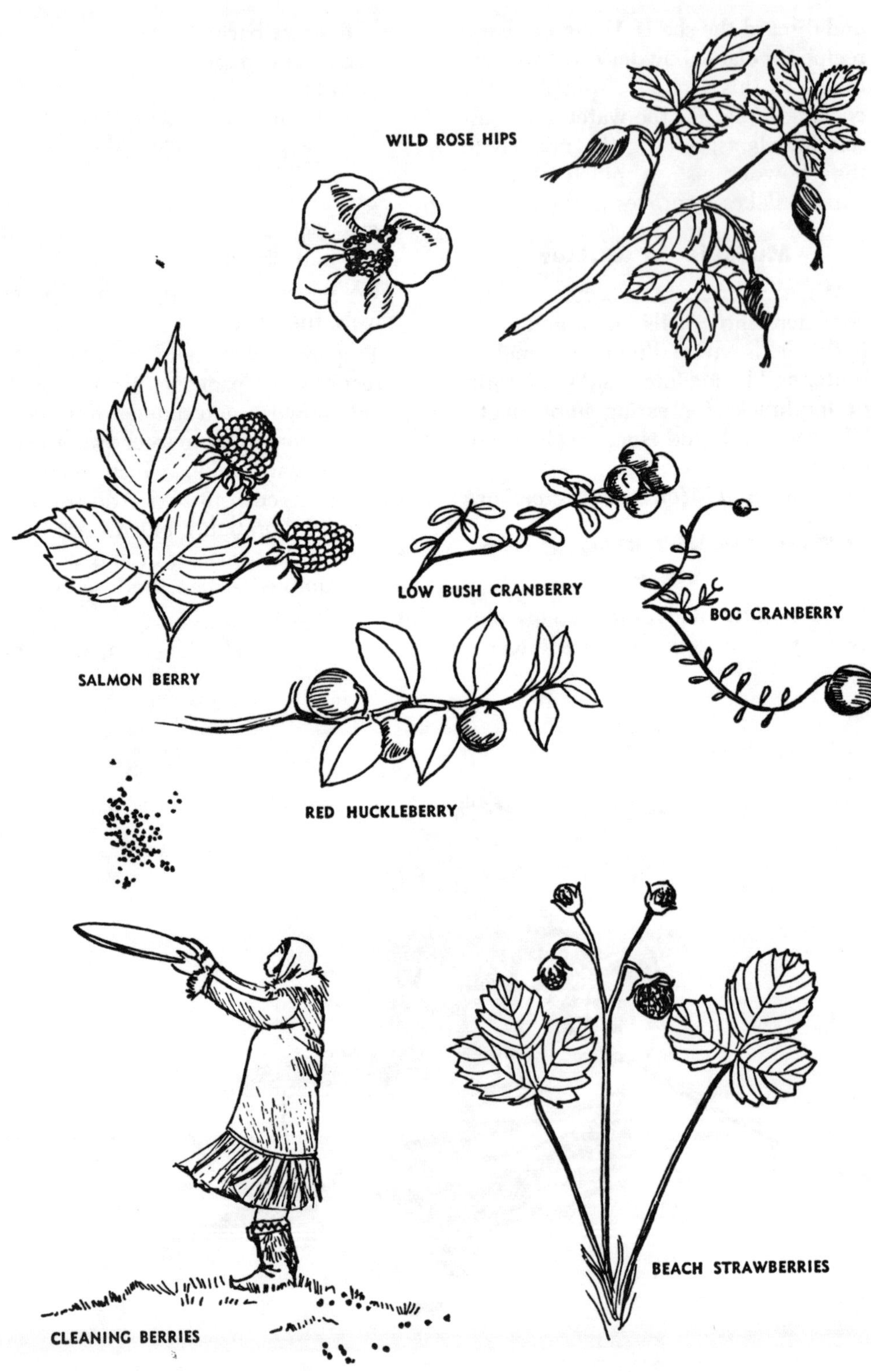
WILD ROSE HIPS
SALMON BERRY
LOW BUSH CRANBERRY
BOG CRANBERRY
RED HUCKLEBERRY
CLEANING BERRIES
BEACH STRAWBERRIES

Chapter 10

WILD FRUITS

Blueberries and Huckleberries

Blueberries and huckleberries belong to the *Vaccinium* family, abundantly represented in Alaska by at least ten members.

Most widespread is the bog blueberry, *V. uliginosum* (grows to two feet, erect and branching stem, flowers light pink and bell-shaped, fruit blue-black and small), common throughout the Interior and the Arctic but only in bogs and alpine meadows in Southeastern Alaska. Common in the Interior, only, is the dwarf blueberry, *V. caespitosa* (whitish flower, fruit large, blue and sweet).

Southeastern Alaska has six tall varieties, including the red huckleberry, *V. parvifolium*, often growing side by side. (What's the difference between a blueberry and a huckleberry? A huckleberry has ten large seeds, a blueberry many small ones. For convenience *V. parvifolium* is called huckleberry — which it is — while all the blue and black varieties are called blueberries—which some are not.)

Some of the tall blueberries follow the coastline to the Alaska Peninsula and the Aleutian Islands. All are used interchangeably in recipes and, where they grow together, are picked into the same bucket (*V. macrophyllum*, a black huckleberry, adds more bulk than flavor).

The lingenberry or lowbush cranberry, abundant in the Interior but scanty in Southeastern Alaska, and the bog cranberry, found throughout the state but nowhere in abundance, are legitimate but distinctive members of the *Vaccinium* family, and are treated as different fruits.

The tall blueberries are the most abundant fruit, wild or domestic, of the Panhandle, and are a fair source of vitamin C. Their season is long. Some ripen in time for "blueberry pie by the Fourth of July," and some last through September or later. They are all "strong" in comparison to the more delicately flavored bog and dwarf blueberries. Thus the Southeastern Alaskan who "loves blueberry pie" will be disappointed if he orders it in Fairbanks, and the farther-northerner will find blueberry jam from the Panhandle too "rich" for his taste. All are considered, by Alaskans at least, vastly superior in flavor to either wild or commercial blueberries from the "South 48."

Southeastern Alaska's midseason (August) blueberries are sometimes hosts to tiny green worms. Huckleberries are less often affected. Some people avoid the worms by avoiding the berries. Others ignore the worms ("just converted blueberries"). To have wormless berries, soak them at least half an hour in salt water (about 1 tbsp. salt to 1 gallon of water). This does not detract from the quality of the fruit, but it brings the worms out so they are easy to see, and the wormy berries can be removed with leaves and other debris. By September the wormy berries have withered and fallen.

To remove blueberry stain from hands, wash thoroughly with soap and cold water, then warm water, then rub with lemon juice or the inside of a lemon rind. Watermelon rind, cucumber and tomato are also effective. To remove stain from clothing or table linen, spread stained side down across a shallow pan in the sink or outdoors. Pour boiling water through stained fabric, swishing it up and down and, if stain is stubborn, let it soak briefly. Almost all fruit stains yield to this treatment. It should be used as soon as convenient. [If stain is very old, or cloth has been washed since it was stained, try boiling or a commercial bleach.]

Blueberry Pie

3 cups blueberries
3 tbsp. flour or minute tapioca
1½ cups sugar
⅛ tsp. salt
1 tbsp. lemon juice
1 tbsp. butter

Mix berries and dry ingredients. [If using frozen berries, allow them to thaw, drain off juice, blend it thoroughly with dry ingredients, then stir in berries—or arrange berries in pie shell and pour on mixture.] Pour into a 9-inch unbaked pie shell, top with the butter, put on top crust. [Crimp edge tight and high to keep juice from boiling out.] Bake 10 minutes at 450°, then lower oven temperature to 350° and bake until juice bubbles up and crust is brown, about 30 minutes.

Blueberry Buckle

Sift together: ½ cup sugar, 2 cups flour, 2½ tsp. baking powder, ¼ tsp. salt.

In a separate bowl beat: 1 egg, ½ cup milk, ¼ cup melted fat.

Pour liquid into dry ingredients and stir just enough to mix. Spread into a shallow glass baking dish (9″ x 9″ x 2″), well greased.

Cover with 1 pint blueberries and 1 tbsp. lemon juice.

Top with a mixture of: ½ cup sugar, 1/3 cup flour, ½ tsp. cinnamon, ¼ cup melted butter.

Bake 50 to 60 minutes at 350°.

University of Alaska
Agricultural Extension Service
College, Alaska

Blueberry Cake

3 tbsp. butter
1 cup sugar
1 egg
1¾ cup flour
2 tsp. baking powder
¾ cup milk
1½ cups blueberries

Sift flour and baking powder together. Combine butter, sugar and egg in bowl and beat. Add milk alternately with flour mixture. Fold in blueberries. Bake until done, about 40 minutes, at 350°.

Serve warm with following sauce:

1 cup blueberries
½ cup water
1 cup sugar
Large lump of butter
Boil 5 minutes and thicken if necessary.

Anne Baltzo, by Mamie Jensen, Juneau

Blueberry Muffins

2 cups flour
¾ cup sugar
4 tsp. baking powder
½ tsp. salt
¼ cup shortening, creamed
1 egg
1 cup milk
1 cup blueberries

Cream shortening, sugar and beaten egg, add sifted dry ingredients, then add milk and stir until blended. Fold in the blueberries lightly. Fill greased muffin tins ¾ full, bake 20 to 25 minutes at 350°.

Marguerite Doucette, Juneau

Blueberry Jam

4½ cups mashed blueberries (about 1½ quarts whole berries)*
7 cups sugar
1 tbsp. lemon juice or vinegar
1 bottle commercial pectin
Dab of butter (to reduce foaming)

Mix berries and sugar thoroughly, add vinegar and butter, bring to a boil on high heat and boil one minute, stirring occasionally as mixture heats and constantly while it boils. Remove from heat, add pectin, stir briefly and skim off any foam, and pour quickly into hot, sterilized jars. Seal. Yield, about 5 pounds.

*If berries are whipped in a blender, most of the seeds will rise to the surface during the boiling and can be skimmed off. Then the skimmings from several batches of jam can be heated and strained through coarse cheesecloth. The resulting product will not be a jelly, but a delicious thick syrup.

It's fun to pick berries on long, sunny summer days; fun to make jam when the days are short and dark, or when it rains. Picked into dry, sterilized, rubber-ring seal jars and sealed promptly, blueberries will keep for a couple of months in a cool, dark place. (The skins become leathery if kept too long.) Frozen with 1 cup of sugar to 1 quart of berries and stored at zero, they may be held indefinitely with no loss of quality. (Be sure to allow for that cup of sugar when making jam from the frozen berries.)

Jam or jelly recipes should never be doubled, but making several batches in succession saves time in assembling equipment and materials and cleaning up afterwards. The kettle (a big one, 6 to 8 quarts, with a narrow flange for easy pouring) and stirring spoon can be used for two batches (but no more) of the same kind of jam or jelly between washings.

Anonymous, Ketchikan

Spiced Blueberry Jam

Boil for 2 minutes:
2 pounds blueberries (4½ cups)
½ tsp. cinnamon
½ tsp. cloves
7 cups sugar
1 bottle commercial pectin

Juice or grated rind of 1 lemon

Remove from fire and add 1 bottle commercial pectin. Skim, pour into sterilized jars, and seal.

University of Alaska
Agricultural Extension Service
College, Alaska

[Those using Southeastern Alaskan blueberries will probably prefer to use only ¼ tsp. cinnamon, ¼ tsp. cloves and 1 tbsp. lemon juice in the above recipe.]

Blueberry Jelly

4 cups juice (takes about 2½ qts. whole berries)
7½ cups sugar
1 tbsp. lemon juice*
1 bottle commercial pectin

Stir sugar and juices thoroughly, bring to a boil over high heat (add a dab of butter to reduce foaming), stirring constantly. Add 1 bottle commercial pectin, boil hard for 1 minute, remove from heat, skim off any foam, pour quickly and seal or cover with hot paraffin at once.

*To dwarf or bog blueberries, add ¼ cup lemon juice.

Anonymous, Ketchikan

Blueberry Sauce

1/3 cup sugar
1½ tbsp. flour
¼ tsp. salt
1 tbsp. lemon juice
1 cup hot water
1 cup blueberries
1 tbsp. butter

Combine sugar, flour and salt. Stir in lemon juice and hot water gradually. Stir until smooth and cook until thickened. Add blueberries and continue to cook until sauce is thick. Remove from fire, add butter and 2 tbsp. rum if you have it handy and like the flavor. Strain and cool. Serve warm or cold, on ice cream or pudding.

Mrs. H. L. Faulkner, Juneau
From B. P. W. COOKBOOK

Blueberry Syrup

2 cups blueberries
1 cup sugar
½ cup water

Combine in a saucepan, boil until berries are soft, then put through a sieve. Seal in pint jars. Use over hot cakes, waffles or biscuits.

Mrs. Mark Jensen, Douglas

Blueberry Conserve

Wash 2 oranges. Cut the rind into thin strips and the sections into slices. Add the juice of 1 lemon, ½ cup water and 1 quart blueberries. Bring to boil and add 2/3 as much sugar. Simmer until thick. Seal in sterilized jars.

Chapter 11

THE RED VACCINIUMS

Huckleberry

The red huckleberry, *Vaccinium parvifolium,* is abundant in Southeastern Alaska. Its fruit, a large, translucent, acid berry, makes jelly of superior flavor and appealing color, and good jam. It also combines well with less easily obtained fruits (as, in Southeastern Alaska, the highbush cranberry), and with fruits (like salal) too strong for the average palate when used alone. Half-and-half is the recommended proportion.

Huckleberries may be used successfully in place of blueberries in the blueberry recipes given in the previous section, but unless berries are very ripe, use five cups of berries instead of four in jam or five cups of juice instead of four in jelly.*

Incidentally, the delicate pink bell-shaped flower of the huckleberry, which blossoms before the leaves appear, is the earliest wildflower in its habitat and may be forced indoors for even earlier blooming.

*To extract juice, add about 1 cup water to 1 quart berries, bring to a boil, simmer gently until color begins to pale, then strain through a jelly bag. To get the most juice and the clearest jelly from any of the lighter-colored berries, put on rubber gloves to protect the hands and squeeze the jelly bag gently until all juice is squeezed out. Then store the juice in the refrigerator for about five days, or bring it to a boil and seal it in hot, sterilized jars. All solids will settle to the bottom. Siphon off the clear juice, being careful not to stir up the thin layer of settlings. Lemon juice for jelly-making should also be extracted several days in advance and allowed to settle, then siphoned off without disturbing the settlings.

Bog Cranberry

Vaccinium oxycoccus, the bog cranberry, is a late fall berry that looks like a small commercial cranberry, may be used in exactly the same way, and tastes the same only better. It grows throughout Alaska, but nowhere in abundance. The threadlike vine creeps through the moss, and picking the berries is a laborious hands-and-knees operation. Any bog cranberry product should be served and savored as a special treat, because of both its superior quality and the effort required to obtain it.

Wherever bog and lowbush cranberries mingle (as they often do in Southeastern Alaska), they should be picked and used together. The combination of two is even more delicious than either by itself.

Lowbush Cranberry

Lowbush cranberry, mountain cranberry, lingenberry, partridgeberry, *tytebeer, nutlut, keepmingyuk, keepmik* and *toomalgleet* are names by which *Vaccinium vitis idaea* is known to people who speak English, Norwegian, Interior Alaska Indian, or Eskimo, and all of them generally regard this berry as the best there is. It is a small red berry that grows in clusters on a low evergreen shrub, in rocky or dry-peaty-acid soil throughout Alaska. It is abundant in most of the state, but sparse in Southeastern Alaska except for a few isolated, little-known and seldom disclosed spots.

The lowbush cranberry may be used in any recipe for commercial cranberries, but it is superior in both color and flavor. It has a high acid content and may be kept, raw or cooked, in a cool place without preserving. A late-ripening berry, it is better picked after the first frost but good even after the snow melts in the spring.

Lowbush Cranberry Sauce

4 cups cranberries, cleaned and washed
2 cups sugar
1 cup water

Place in saucepan and boil until the skins pop, about 20 minutes. Taste, and if you prefer a sweeter sauce, add more sugar. Store in a cool place. It would keep indefinitely, but won't last long after you start to eat it!

Betty Snider, Anchorage

Cran-Ban Pie

2 c. lowbush cranberries (cooked into sauce or canned)
3 egg yolks
1 tbsp. cornstarch
2 tbsp. butter
1 tbsp. vanilla
3 ripe bananas
9″ pie shell, baked

Boil cranberry sauce 1 minute. Mix egg yolks, cornstarch and salt (add beaten yolks to dry ingredients, stirring constantly), then add hot berry sauce very slowly, continuing to stir vigorously. Return to heat, keep on stirring, and cook until thick. Remove from heat and add butter, vanilla and a small pinch of salt. Cool. Slice bananas, then pour a layer of cranberry mixture into pie shell, cover with bananas, and cover bananas with remaining sauce immediately. Top with your favorite meringue and bake 15 minutes in slow oven (325° F.) until meringue is lightly browned.

Louise Juhnke, Chugiak

Wild Cranberries

1 pair hip boots for kneeling in cold swamp
1 bail bucket slipped over strong belt
1 afternoon digging in wet moss for cranberries, not too ripe. Pick over.

Wash in cold water and let dry on paper. Grind in food chopper. Add 1 cup granulated sugar to 1 cup berry pulp. Place in stone jar, stir occasionally till sugar dissolves (do not cook), keep in cool, dry storage and serve with turkey, other fowl or meat.

Crystal Snow Jenne, Juneau
From BPW COOKBOOK

Cranberry Marlowe

Melt 20 marshmallows in ½ c. milk in top of a double boiler over rapidly boiling water. Cook 1½ c. cranberries with ¼ c. sugar and ½ c. water until soft, about 20 minutes. Strain through sieve and add to marshmallow mixture. When cool, fold in 1 c. cream whipped until stiff. Place in tray of refrigerator or pack in salt and ice (equal parts) and freeze 3 to 4 hours. Serves 6.

Anonymous, Ketchikan

Raw Cranberry Salad

2 pkgs. lemon Jello
3 cups boiling water
½ cup sugar
1 cup crushed pineapple, drained
1 cup finely chopped celery
2 apples, diced
1 orange, diced
Juice and rind of 1 lemon
½ cup nutmeats
4 cups lowbush cranberries (may be put through coarse grinder)

Pour hot water over the Jello and add the sugar. Stir till dissolved. When it begins to jell add the remaining ingredients. Chill and serve.

Cranberry Conserve

Slice very thin 1 lemon and ½ orange and cook in a small amount of water until soft, about 5 minutes. Mix 2 cups water, 2 cups sugar and 2 cups lowbush cranberries together and boil rapidly for 5 to 10 minutes. Add the lemon-orange mixture and boil till clear and thick, then add about ½ cup nutmeats. Pour into sterilized jars and seal.

Cranberry Marmalade

3 lb. carrots, ground fine
2 oranges, ground or sliced fine
1 lemon sliced very fine

Mix together in saucepan, bring to a full rolling boil, then add 2 cups sugar and 1 pint cranberries and cook 5 minutes more. Stir well, pour into sterilized jars and seal.

Highbush Cranberries

Viburnum edule, commonly called highbush cranberry, is not a cranberry and doesn't look like one. It is a small, waxy red or orange-red berry with a single large, flat stone. It grows on a tall (up to eight or ten feet), often scraggly bush with slender gray branches and opposite leaves shaped much like a maple leaf. It ripens in early fall, but for best flavor and higher acid content it should be picked just before it is fully ripe and before the first frost. It grows almost anywhere in Alaska south of the Arctic Circle, but is rare in Southeastern Alaska. There it is found only beside fresh water, in widely scattered spots apparently well known to the local bears, and must be gathered early or bears strip the bushes clean.

In both flavor and odor the highbush cranberry is different from anything else—strongly reminiscent of the deep wilderness, the perfect complement to game meats—and it is esteemed very highly or not at all. (Used with huckleberry, apple, rhubarb, currant, rose hip or raspberry, it is usually palatable to those who find it too "gamy" when undiluted. When the highbush cranberry is plentiful, it is often used to extend less plentiful fruits.) It makes a beautiful jelly with excellent texture, and is prized for fruit catsup and beverages, but because of the large seed is not suitable for jam, sauce or pie.

To extract the juice: Add 3 cups water to 2 cups berries, simmer for about 5 minutes, mashing berries while they simmer, and strain through a jelly bag.

To make jelly: use commercial pectin and follow the recipe for currant jelly, or use 2/3 cup sugar to 1 cup juice and boil until jelly stage is reached.

Cranberry Catsup

Cook until soft: 1 lb. onions chopped fine, 4 lb. (8 cups) highbush cranberries, 2 cups water. Rub through a coarse sieve. Add 2 cups vinegar, 4 cups sugar, 1 tbsp. each of ground cloves, cinnamon, allspice, salt, celery seed and pepper. Boil until thick, pour into sterilized jars and seal. Serve with poultry, meat or baked beans.

Cranberry-Apple Butter

Soak 1 lb. dried apples in 2 qts. warm water for 1 hour. Add 2 qts. highbush cranberries and cook until soft. Put through a coarse sieve. Reheat and add ¾ as much sugar, 1 tsp. cinnamon, ¼ tsp. salt, ½ tsp. cloves. Cook until clear. Add juice and grated rind of 1 lemon. Pack in sterilized jars and seal.

Cranberry-Rhubarbade

Simmer and mash together: 1 qt. cranberries, 1 qt. finely cut rhubarb, 3 cups water. Strain through wet jelly bag. Add 1 cup sugar to each quart of juice. Heat to 170° F. for 1 minute. Pour into sterilized bottles, cap, cool quickly and store in a cool, dark place.

University of Alaska
Agricultural Extension Service

Highbush Cranberry Wine

To 4 qts. crushed berries add 2 qts. warm, boiled water and let stand for three days. Strain and measure. Add 2 gallons water and 3 pounds sugar to each gallon of strained liquor. Put in jars, loosely covered, and store in a dark, warm place.

Jeanne Woods, Palmer

Cranberry-Pineapple Butter

3 cups high- or lowbush cranberries, 1 cup crushed pineapple, 3½ cups sugar. Mix thoroughly and boil until it thickens. Pour into hot, sterilized jars and seal.

Marie Westenbarger, Palmer

The Rubus Family

Rubus idaeus, the red raspberry, grows wild in parts of Alaska, particularly in the Anchorage-Matanuska and Fairbanks areas, where it is abundant enough to provide a substantial source of vitamin C. It can be used exactly like the domestic varieties.

Rubus pedatus, the trailing raspberry, grows on the Panhandle, across the gulf coast to the Alaska Peninsula, the Aleutian Islands and Kodiak, and in the upper Yukon Valley. It has an excellent flavor and makes a delicious jelly, but is rarely found in quantity.

Rubus arcticus, the nagoonberry, grows as a single red berry on a short stem, from a spreading underground root, and ripens in late summer. It is found, but exceedingly sparsely, on the Panhandle and in the Interior, and is highly prized for jelly.

Rubus chamaemorus, the cloudberry or baked appleberry, grows singly on a short, two- or three-leafed stem from a creeping root. When ripe, in late August to mid-September, it is amber in color. It is found on the Panhandle, but is abundant mainly from Seward Peninsula south and east to the Kuskokwim River basin. The Eskimos of this area gather it in large quantities and store it in sealskin pokes or kegs in their ice cellars, then eat it during the winter with seal oil or sugar, or both. It may also be used like strawberries. As a source of vitamin C, the uncooked and unfermented cloudberry is two to three times as high as its weight in orange.

Rubus spectabilis, the salmonberry, grows on the southern coast from the Panhandle to the Aleutian Islands and on Kodiak, and ripens in late summer. Bush and fruit look like a robust raspberry, though the fruit on neighboring bushes may be bright yellow or dark red. The yellow is said to have the better flavor but the difference is scant. Both have a slight bitterness which "grows on one," like the taste of ripe olives.

To serve raw, pick berries with an inch or more of stem, wash only if necessary, arrange on a large plate with a bowl of sugar in the middle, and garnish with salmonberry leaves.

For jelly, extract juice and proceed as for raspberry jelly. (Salmonberry is not recommended for jam because of the large seeds.)

For preserves, stem and hull the berries, add an equal amount of sugar, heat slowly to dissolve the sugar, simmer for 15 minutes, then remove the berries. Boil the juice for 15 minutes longer, add the berries, pack into hot, sterilized jars and seal.

Rubus parviflorus, the thimbleberry, grows on the Panhandle and is said to be a favorite of the aborigines, but persons who have used this berry elsewhere find the Alaskan variety insipid to the taste and seldom gather it.

Other Wild Fruits

The crowberry, *Empertrum nigrum,* is a very dark berry with a silvery sheen that grows from the Panhandle to the Arctic on a low, trailing evergreen shrub with needle-like leaves. As the raw berry is mealy and tasteless it is usually ignored, but with a dash of lemon juice added it makes a tasty jelly or pie, and it combines well with other fruits, especially blueberry.

Salal, *Gaultheria shallon,* grows in Southeastern Alaska, on a robust laurel-like evergreen bush. The fruit, like small Concord grapes in spike-like clusters, is very juicy when ripe. To use, snip off the clusters with scissors and extract the juice. It has a faint onion flavor, but combined with huckleberry juice it makes an appetizing jelly.

The red currant, *Ribes triste,* grows in much of Alaska from Skagway north and west to the Kobuk River. It is easily identified by anyone familiar with the cultivated currant, and may be used in the same way.

Related species include: *R. laxiflorum,* trailing black currant, found on the Panhandle and the Kenai and in central Alaska. It is especially good in a conserve with orange and lemon *R. hudsonianum,* the northern black currant, is found in the Interior but considered scarcely edible. *R. bracteosum,* the blue currant, found in Southeastern Alaska, is gathered by the Indians, who mix it with salmon roe and store it for winter use. *R. glan-*

dulosum, the fetid currant, is a red berry on a bristly bush, found throughout central Alaska but seldom utilized.

Ribes oxyconthoides, the gooseberry, is found in the Interior and used like domestic gooseberries. *R. lacustre,* the swamp gooseberry, grows from the Alaska Peninsula northward. It has a bristly, purplish-black berry, edible but unattractive in appearance and odor.

Of wild strawberries there are two varieties: *Fragaria chileonsis,* or beach strawberry is found along the coast from Southeastern Alaska to Seward Peninsula, is up to an inch long, and in some spots (particularly Gustavus and Strawberry Point) grows in real abundance. *F. glauca,* the Yukon strawberry, is found in the Interior. It is smaller, but worth gathering. Both are easily recognized, endowed with the eating quality and high vitamin C content of domestic strawberries, and used in the same ways.

Rose Hip

The hip, haw or seed pod of the rose, seldom regarded as a food, is one of the best sources of vitamin C to be found (three hips yield as much vitamin C as a whole orange) and in Alaska, where such things as tomatoes and oranges are expensive, if available, nature has generously provided two varieties of wild roses—*Rosa acicularis* (prickly rose, or *neechee* to the Indians) from the southern coast to the Yukon River, and *R. nutkana* (Nutka rose) on the coast from Juneau and Sitka to Unalaska. These and the cultivated species develop large red hips of value as food even after they are dried, or have hung on the bushes all winter.

Collect rose hips preferably after the first frost, when they are red and ripe but still firm, and prepare as soon as convenient. Wash, remove the "brushes," barely cover with water, and simmer for 15 minutes. Extract the juice and use it for jelly or syrup. Sieve the pulp and use it for jams, fruit catsup and so forth. The flavor needs a lift from some tart fruit such as lingenberry.

To dry rose hips, cut in two, remove seeds, dry quickly in a cool oven or warming closet, pulverize if you like, and add to beverages, cooked fruit, bread, cookies, anything to get them eaten. Collected soon after ripening, prepared without overcooking and used generously, rose hips may be relied upon to supply all the vitamin C needed in the normal diet.

DON'T EAT!

Actaea ruba (red-berried) and *A. eburnea* (white-berried), known as baneberry, snakeberry or mooseberry, are to be found and avoided on most of the southern coast and in the upper Yukon valley. The plant is a perennial with a thick rootstock, smooth or slightly hairy stems, two to four feet high, with large, thin, coarsely toothed and usually lobed leaves divided into three leaflets. Flowers, in spike-like clusters, are small and white; fruit is a round red or white several-seeded berry on a thick stalk, red on the white-berried *A. eburnea.*

The quality of this berry is not debatable; it's poisonous. As few as half a dozen berries will make you sick, and a few more will end your berry-picking forever.

Chapter 12

WILD VEGETABLES

Mushroom-Corn Casserole

2 cans cream-style corn
1 egg
½ cup cream or condensed milk
1 pint shaggy mane mushrooms, well drained*
Salt and pepper

Beat egg well, add corn, cream, salt and pepper. Place half this mixture in greased casserole, arrange mushrooms on top and cover with remainder of corn mixture. Dot with butter and bake 30-40 minutes at 350° F.

*Shaggy manes, if fresh, should be fried first in a little butter (they really stew) as they are very moist and precooking will remove most of the excess moisture.

Creamed Mushrooms

This is best made with Boletus or field mushrooms. Shaggy manes are too moist.

Brown mushrooms in butter. Add 1 cup chicken broth and simmer for a few minutes. Season with salt, pepper and a dash of paprika. Thicken as for any creamed dish. Add 1 cup sour cream and stir thoroughly. Remove from heat. Serve over hot, buttered toast, wild rice or brown rice.

Mrs. Vic Power, Juneau

Mushroom Casserole

Sauté 1 quart mushrooms; combine with 1 cup whitesauce; add 1 tbsp. chopped chives, 2 tbsp. chopped pimento, 1 tbsp. chopped mint, ¼ tsp. dry mustard. Turn into greased casserole, cover with 1 cup grated cheese, sprinkle with breadcrumbs. Bake 10 to 15 minutes to melt the cheese.

Mushroom Goulash with Eggplant

Combine 4 large mushrooms, chopped; 1 diced eggplant,* 1 cup tomatoes, 2 green peppers, 1 clove garlic; simmer in 3 tbsp. fat; season with salt, pepper and marjoram. Cook for 20 minutes.

*A quart of diced, cooked vegetables, any combination, may be substituted for the eggplant. Try carrots,

AMANITA PANTHERINA (POISONOUS)
BOLETUS AMABILIS (EDIBLE)
ROZITES CAPERATA (EDIBLE)

turnips, cabbage, potatoes, peas and onions.

Pickled Mushrooms

Select 2 cups small button mushrooms. Add 1 tsp. salt, 2 bay leaves, 1 clove garlic, sliced. Cover with 1 cup hot vinegar boiled with one sprig tarragon. Let stand 3 days before using.

Agricultural Extension Service
University of Alaska
College, Alaska

Dandelion Greens de Luxe

Pick, clean and wash two quarts or a little more of young dandelions. Buds that are not too tall or in flower may be used, if greens are young and tender.

Boil in salted water, as for spinach, until greens are nearly done, then set to drain.

Hard-boil 3 eggs. Dice 3 slices of bacon and fry it in a large, heavy skillet until crisp and brown.

Beat together 2 eggs, 4 tbsp. vinegar, ¼ cup milk, ½ tsp. dry mustard and salt and sugar to taste. (If you like your greens on the sour side, omit the sugar.)

Add the drained greens to the hot, crisp bacon and fat in the skillet, pour on the dressing, stir thoroughly and cook until greens are tender. Slice hard-cooked eggs over the top and serve. Also good cold.

Dan "Rudy" Rudisill, Anchorage

Goosetongue

(*Plantago maritima,* or seaside plantain)

Goosetongue should be picked when young, in May or June.

Pick young leaves and wash in fresh water or clean sea water. Chop some bacon and onion, fry the bacon, and brown the onion in the drippings. Add the goosetongue and enough water to steam it. Cover and cook about 10 minutes. Serve with butter, salt and pepper.

Goosetongue, which has a delicious tart flavor, may also be used in a mixed vegetable salad.

Mrs. E. E. Weschenfelder, Fritz Cove

Goose grass or seashore plantain, *Plantago macrocarpa,* looks much like goosetongue but has longer, more slender leaves. It can be used like goosetongue, but is usually considered inferior to it.

Wild Cucumber

(*Streptopus amplexifolius,* clasping twisted stalk)

Gather in the spring, when stalks are no thicker than your little finger. Use leaves and stalk, cut up like green onions, in mixed salad. They have a fresh, cucumber-like flavor.

To cook: Wash greens in fresh water or clean sea water. Lift out of the washing water without shaking, place in kettle, add ½ tsp. salt, cover and steam as you would spinach, for about 15 minutes. (No water need be added.) Serve with butter, salt and pepper. The flavor, when cooked, is faintly like asparagus—most delicious.

Mrs. E. E. Weschenfelder, Fritz Cove

Caribou Moss

This recipe is thousands of years old and is still used in Alaska. It is the only known method of eating caribou moss successfully, and is guaranteed to prevent scurvy.

Kill a caribou, leave the first stomach alone for three days, then open it, take out the contents and use it like sauerkraut. Stomach content may be used when caribou is first killed, but is not as good.

Lee Hancock, Anchorage

Lesser-Known Greens

Wild celery, *Angelica lucida* (Eskimo names, *Ahzeeahlook* and *Egoosuk).* Gather young stems and tender leaf stalks, peel and eat raw. Cook the leaves for a green vegetable. Flavor like unbleached celery.

Kamchatka rock-cress, *Arabis lyrata.* Collect rosettes of lobed leaves in spring and add to tossed salads or cook and serve as a green vegetable. Radish-like flavor.

Seabeach sandwort or sea-chickweed, *Arenaria peploides.* Gather leaves before plant flowers. Eaten raw, they are a good source of vitamins A and C. Used by Eskimos, chopped and cooked with other greens and allowed to sour, then sometimes mixed with reindeer fat and berries to make "Eskimo Ice Cream."

Winter cress, *Barbarea orthoceras,* one of the earliest spring greens available. Collect leaf rosettes of the first year's growth (this is a biennial) and cook or use raw in salad. Somewhat bitter radish-like flavor.

Marsh marigold or cowslip, *Caltha palustris. Do not eat raw.* Raw leaves contain a poison, helleborin, which is destroyed by cooking. Collect leaves and smooth stems before the flowers appear. The long white roots are sometimes gathered and boiled for eating.

Lambsquarter, *Chenopodium album,* an introduced species. Collect in early summer, cook in small amount of water, don't overcook. Furnishes significant amounts of vitamins A and C if used soon after gathering and not overcooked.

Strawberry blite or Indian strawberry, *Chenopodium capitatum.* Gather tender young leaves in summer, use raw in salad or cook like garden spinach. Good source of vitamins A and C if used promptly and not overcooked.

Siberian spring beauty, *Claytonia sibirica.* Collect tender leaves in spring; use raw in mixed salad or cook briefly in small amount of water.

Spoonwort or scurvy grass, *Cochlearia officinalis,* found on beaches of the entire Alaskan coast. Collect entire plant in spring or early summer, young rosettes of new plants in fall. Use raw or cooked.

Spreading wood fern, *Dryopteris spinulosa,* and western bracken, *Pteridium aquilinum,* may be collected in the young or "fiddleneck" stage and steamed and served like asparagus. The old leaf stalks on the underground stem of the wood fern are customarily roasted, peeled and eaten by Indians of Southeastern Alaska and the Eskimos of Bristol Bay and the lower Kuskokwim. The full-grown fronds of bracken are tough, and develop a poison.

Fireweed, *Epilobium angustifolium,* common in most of the state, is collected in the young-shoot stage. Cook briefly in a small amount of salted water and serve like asparagus; blanch in boiling water and serve with French dressing; or peel and eat raw. Becomes tough and bitter as the plant matures.

Dwarf fireweed or rock rose, *Epilobium latifolium,* also found throughout the state, is collected in early summer and used as a salad green.

Labrador or Hudson's Bay tea,

Ledum groenlandicum. Has strongly aromatic leaves which are steeped into a palatable tea. Believed to be a cathartic if used in large quantities. *Ledum decumbens*, a smaller plant with needle-like leaves, is used in the same way.

Sea lovage or wild celery, *Ligusticum hultenii,* may be collected before the plant flowers. Leaves and stalks may be eaten raw, like celery, or cooked as a green vegetable.

Poisonous Plants and Actaea eburnea

Baneberry, *Actaea rubra*—thick rootstock, stems smooth or slightly hairy, leaves large, divided into three leaflets, white flowers in spike-like clusters, fruit a white or red several-seeded berry; height two to four feet. Deadly poisonous.

Narcissus-flowered anemone, *Anemone narcissiflora.* Early spring growth on the upper end of the root is sometimes eaten, but some members of this plant family contain anemonine, a mildly poisonous substance.

Poison water hemlock, *Cicuta mackenziana, C. Maculata and C. Douglasii,* perennial up to seven feet high, stout, jointed, reddish stem hollow between the joints; leaf-stalks sheath the stem; leaves alternate, divided into narrow leaflets up to four inches long, with toothed edges; small white flowers in umbrella-like clusters. Grows in wet meadows and beside streams and lakes from Southeastern Alaska north to the Brooks Range. A very small portion of the root will cause death within a few hours; poison present but not so concentrated in the remainder of the plant. There is some chance of survival if free vomiting can be produced promptly, followed by a cathartic.

Wild sweet pea, *Hedysarum mackenzii,* up to one and a half feet tall, stems erect and minutely hairy; leaves in small, rounded leaflets, smooth above, grayish-hairy underneath; flowers rose to purple, showy and fragrant. Reported to be toxic.

False hellebore, *Veratrum eschscholtzii,* a stout-stemmed perennial, up to eight feet high, thick rootstock, alternate leaves broadly oval with pointed tip, clasping the stem; small greenish flowers in large, spikelike clusters; fruit a three-celled capsule. Plant causes death by asphyxia.

Death camus, *Zygadenus elegans:* a bulb perennial somewhat resembling the narcissus plant, with smooth, leafy stems up to two feet high; alternate, long, narrow, flat leaves clasp stem; three-petal, greenish-white flowers in loose terminal clusters; fruit a capsule. Found in most of the Interior. All parts of this plant are deadly, causing salivation, nausea, vomiting, lowered temperature, breathing difficulty and coma.

Kelp

The giant kelp is easily recognized by the floating bulb attached to a long, hollow stem, rooted to the bottom in shallow bays or channels. Gather during June, July or August, and use only the rooted tubes (and bulbs). Wash and peel (a vegetable peeler is easier to use for this than a paring knife), and use like green tomatoes or cucumbers in pickles and relish. Kelp may also be used as a substitute for watermelon rind in preserves. [The flavor and texture of pickled kelp do not improve with age, but begin to deteriorate after a few months.]

Alaska Sweet Sea Pickles

4 pounds bulb kelp
1 cup salt
2 gallons water
½ tsp. alum
2 qts. water
3½ cups sugar
1 pint white vinegar
½ tsp. oil of cloves
½ tsp. oil of cinnamon

Cut kelp in 12-inch lengths and split bulbs. Pare off dark surface layer. Soak kelp 2 hours in a brine solution prepared by dissolving 1 cup salt in 2 gallons of water. Be sure to keep kelp covered with brine. Remove from brine and wash thoroughly with cold water.

Cut kelp into 1-inch cubes, or slice in rings about ¼ inch thick, and soak in alum solution (½ tsp. alum to 2 qts. cold water) 15 minutes. Drain and wash in cold water, drain again, place in enamel kettle and cover with boiling water. Cook only until kelp can be pierced with a fork. Drain.

Combine sugar, vinegar and oils; boil 2 minutes; pour over cooked kelp. Let stand overnight in an enamel kettle or crock. In the morning drain off syrup and reheat it to boiling, pour back over kelp and allow to stand 24 hours. On third morning, heat both kelp and syrup to boiling, pack in jars and seal while hot. Makes 3 pints.

(When oil of cinnamon and oil of cloves are used, kelp remains clear and almost transparent. A small amount of green food coloring may be used to give better color. If whole spices are used, tie them in small bag.)

Chapter **13**

SOURDOUGH

Sourdough Starter

Mix 1 cup flour, 1 cup water, ½ to 1 package (or cake) of yeast in a pint jar. Let stand in a warm place overnight.

Sponge

Empty starter into a bowl. Fill the pint jar with warm water (2 cups), empty it into the bowl, add 2 cups flour and beat to a smooth batter. Let bowl stand in a warm place overnight. Batter should be thin enough to pour. If too thick, add a little warm water.

In the morning, take out ¼ to ½ cup of the sponge, put in clean pint jar, and place in refrigerator or cool place for the next sponge.

A sourdough starter will be good for many years if kept in a cool place and used every week. Never add anything to the starter except flour and water.

To carry the starter or keep it longer than a week, thicken it with flour to form a ball and keep it in the flour or in a covered container. To activate it, thin it out with water.

Sourdough Hot Cakes

To the sponge (which should be about 3 cups after a portion has been put aside for starter) add 2 unbeaten eggs (or ¼ cup dried egg powder mixed with 1/3 cup water). Sprinkle over the top 1 tbsp. sugar, 1 tsp. soda, 1 tsp. salt, 1 tbsp. oil or melted fat. Beat with a fork until foamy. If very thick, add a small amount of water or milk. Bake on a hot griddle.

Sourdough Waffles

To the sponge (not including portion set aside for starter) add: 1 tsp. salt, 2 tbsp. sugar, 1 tsp. soda, 2 unbeaten eggs and ¼ cup melted fat. Mix well with a fork or slit spoon. Bake like other waffles.

Sourdough Muffins

Sift together: 1 cup fine whole wheat flour, 1 tsp. soda, 1 tsp. salt and ¼ cup sugar. Measure 2 cups sourdough sponge and add 2 eggs (unbeaten) and 1/3 cup melted fat. Mix well. Add flour mixture. If too thick to pour, add a little water; if too thin, add a little flour. Spoon into greased muffin tins and bake at 400° F. for 15 to 20 minutes. Makes 12 large or 18 small muffins.

Sourdough Bread (Brown)

To 1 cup sourdough sponge add 1 tsp. salt, 2 tbsp. molasses and 2 tbsp. fat. Mix well. Add 2 cups coarse graham flour, or enough to make a stiff dough. Knead lightly. Place in warm greased loaf tin, let stand ½ hour, then bake at 375° F. until lightly browned, about 40 minutes. This is a coarse, heavy bread with a good flavor.

Sourdough Bread (White)

Use the above recipe, substituting white flour for graham flour and omitting the molasses.

Yeast Ferment Bread

Where fresh yeast is not readily available, a yeast ferment may be started with dry yeast foam or granulated yeast. Alaskans have been known to keep a yeast ferment "starter" going for years without buying new yeast. A yeast ferment started (or activated) the day before bread is to be baked gives results as rapid as those of fresh yeast. One cup of good, foamy starter is equal to one cake of fresh yeast. Always save 1 cup starter to use for the next batch of bread. Keep it *cool but not frozen* until the day before the bread is to be baked. If without refrigeration, bake bread at least twice a week in warm weather to keep starter sweet. If starter turns moldy or has an off odor, throw it away and begin again.

Yeast Ferment or Starter

Wash, pare and boil one medium-large potato, drain and save the water. Or, cook potatoes for a meal, save one, and save the water. Mash the potato, add the potato water and 1 level tbsp. sugar, and cool to lukewarm. Add 1 package granulated yeast or 1 cake yeast, crumbled. Add lukewarm water if necessary to make 1 quart of mixture. Mix well, cover loosely, and keep in a comfortably warm place (85° to 90° F.) until next morning. If potato water is unsalted the starter will work faster.

To activate this starter bring it to room temperature the day before bread is to be baked, add 1 level tbsp. sugar, 1 mashed potato, lukewarm potato water plus enough lukewarm water to make 1 quart, and (as when setting the original starter) keep it in a warm place overnight.

Bread

Next morning this yeast ferment should be bubbly or frothy. If it seems cold, set it in tepid water until barely lukewarm (80° to 85° F.). If flour seems cold, warm slightly, but do not heat. Ingredients should feel only lukewarm to the hand.

Measure 10 cups (3 lbs.) sifted flour and 4 level tsps. salt into a mixing bowl. Dissolve ¼ cup sugar in yeast mixture, save 1 cup for starter, add rest to flour mixture and blend, then add 4 level tbsps. melted (but not hot) shortening. Mix all together in the bowl, then turn out on floured board (not a cold board) to knead.

Knead, with greased hands, for five minutes, adding a little flour to the board from time to time if bread is sticky. Knead from the outside in, moving mass of dough clockwise with one hand while kneading with the other, in short, rhythmic motions. All flour should be worked in at this time as adding more later will make dark streaks in the bread. When dough "squeaks" and outside surface is completely smooth, kneading is complete.

Shape into a ball, grease top lightly, place in a large, lightly greased bowl, cover lightly and put in a warm place (85° F.) free from drafts, and let rise until it has doubled in bulk and retains a dent when pressed lightly. Knead lightly and allow to rise again (this step may be omitted), then shape into loaves and place in greased bread pans. Handle dough quickly and lightly at this point; don't knead it back to its original bulk. Newly molded loaf should about half-fill pan. Grease top to prevent crusting. Put pans in warm place and allow dough to rise until center of the loaf is a little higher than the top of the pan.

Preheat oven to 400° F. Put in bread and after 10 minutes reduce heat to 375° (in a coal or wood stove, 325° to 350° is better). A cup of water in the oven during baking helps form a tender crust. Bake 45 to 50 minutes for one-pound loaf, one hour or more for larger loaves. Remove from pan at once and cool on a wire rack. (Cold air blowing over the hot loaf will cause the crust to crack.)

University of Alaska
Agricultural Extension Service

Sourdough Starter without Yeast

Use a stone crock with a cover. Stir ½ cup sugar into 1 quart lukewarm water. Add enough flour to make a thin batter, about 3 cups. Mix thoroughly and put in a warm place for about a week. Listen to the hissing noise and when the batter is working fast, keep it down by stirring it every day.

To use, pour off about 1 cup batter, cover the remainder with a tight lid, and keep the mixture going by adding more flour and water from time to time.

Sourdough Pancakes

To 1 cup sourdough (above) add 2 eggs, ¼ cup melted butter or bacon drippings, 1 tbsp. sugar, ½ tsp. salt, 1 tsp. soda dissolved in 1 tbsp. hot water. Stir, and watch so it doesn't go over the edge of the bowl. Pour this thin batter onto hot, greased griddle, and when crisp edges curl and top is bubbly, flip over. Serve with blueberry syrup for a real treat.

Anonymous

Polenta

3 medium-sized potatoes, diced fine (about 2½ cups)
1 qt. water
2 tsp. salt
¾ cup yellow cornmeal

Put water and salt in deep kettle, bring to a boil, add potatoes and bring to a boil again. Add cornmeal very slowly, stirring all the while. Cook over low heat for 45 minutes, stirring constantly (or cook in double-boiler), taking care to avoid scorching. When stiff, turn onto buttered platter or into buttered casserole or ring mold (2 qt. size). Use instead of potatoes, rice, or what-not as a base for gravy, creamed chicken and so forth. Very good with browned mooseburger and gravy.

Louise Juhnke, Chugiak

Unleavened Bread

5 cups flour

1 tbsp. sugar
1 tbsp. salt
Water

Mix flour, sugar and salt with as little water as possible to make a stiff dough. Knead and pull lively until smooth. Roll out as thin as soda crackers, score, and bake in 12 by 12 inch sheets at 350° until barely brown, 8 to 12 minutes.

Charles Ricci, Spenard

Pone

4 cups cornmeal
1½ tsp. salt
3 cups hot water

Mix together and stir vigorously. The harder you stir, the lighter the pone. Press into thin cakes (¼ to ½ inch thick) and bake in a reflector oven or fry in hot fat (just a little fat). If baking, cooking time will be about 35 minutes; if frying, about 12 minutes. Serves two or three.

Charles Ricci, Spenard

Flour Mixture for Campers

10 pounds white flour
10 pounds whole wheat flour
5 pounds yellow cornmeal
4 pounds soy flour
4 pounds wheat germ

Mix thoroughly in a large container, then pack in heavy pliofilm bags. This mixture can be used for all flour requirements in camp, and is wholesome and nourishing.

Mardy Murie, Moose, Wyoming

STARTING A NEW SOURDOUGH POT, KEEP IT WARM

YOUR PERSONAL RECIPES
(and others you might "borrow")

YOUR PERSONAL RECIPES
(and others you might "borrow")

YOUR PERSONAL RECIPES
(and others you might "borrow")

YOUR PERSONAL RECIPES
(and others you might "borrow")